GOD PROTECTS THE IGNORANT... SOMETIMES

The Memoirs of One Pilot's Journey - Missions in Vietnam, Iran, and on Rescue Missions

by Jim Stills

God Protects the Ignorant... Sometimes

By Jim Stills

Copyright (c) 2007

All rights reserved.

Fifth Estate Publishers,

Post Office Box 116, Blountsville, AL 35031

First Printing 2007

Edited by Jeannie Dimter and Rachel Metzler

Cover Design by T. S.. Carson and An Quigley

Printed on acid-free paper

Library of Congress Control No: 2007922054

ISBN: 1-933580-33X

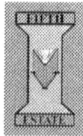

Fifth Estate   2007

Dedication

To Paulette, my wife, who stood by me through throat cancer, broken leg and many minor surgeries. In addition I wish to thank Dr. Vic, my good friend, for all of his support in the real estate deals over the last 17 years.

Publisher's Comment

Written in his own humorous, Southern voice, Jim Stills leads us through his funny, sad, and tragic adventures in Vietnam, Iran, and back to the U.S. where he continued as a helicopter pilot for Life Saver rescue missions. Jim's compassion for others is balanced by his ability to see the irony and divine hand of God at work in life. His stories are insightful, uplifting, and inspiring. War is indeed hell, but it also carries the hopes and spontaneous levity which flows from the human heart.

Joseph Lumpkin
Fifth Estate Publisher

INTRODUCTION

I'm beginning this story in this way because every book I have read has had a boring section or chapter. I'm going to try to eliminate most of the boredom and get on to the meat of the episodes. I was born in Eastern Tennessee, next to the North Carolina Border. If you are familiar with the area, you know that is mountain country. Most of my relatives were in the beverage business. I think that's how I got the name Stills.

I have heard people talk about being poor but, as of this date, I have not heard of any that were any worse off than my family. We did not have running water or electricity until I was five years old, when my folks moved to Ohio; boy, was I happy. At least I had the opportunity to get somewhat of an education: high school, the army, flight school, and Vietnam.

Most of these events I want to tell you about occurred over there. A few events were on this side of the pond. The things I would like to share are serious but some are humorous, now that I have had time to evaluate the situation. I hope you enjoy these memories, as I will try to pass them on without fluffing them up too badly.

As I write about all these life happenings, I start to reminisce about all the close calls I've had. I can remember at the age of 3 or 4 when I was going fishing with my father behind my grandma's house, at the creek. As we were walking through the field (and I was in front), there, a few feet away, was a rattlesnake all curled up with his tail rattling. Of course, I froze, and all of a sudden I heard a thump; and my dad had chunked a rock on the snake's head. This was the first time I recalled that "God Protects the Ignorant".

The second time was real brilliant. My friend and I hiked into the woods to find a suitable tree to build a tree house. After we found what we thought was the perfect tree, we got started.

First thing was to clear bushes from around the tree so we could get to it easily. We hacked off the bushes with a hatchet which left 8 or 10 inch stakes everywhere. Finally, we got the floor built and started hanging the rope ladder. We got the ladder hung and I started my way up. I got about 8 or 10 feet high and the rope started to stretch, then it broke, and I fell flat on my back. After I realized what had happened, I saw I had stakes on both sides of my head, under my armpits, and around my legs and groin area, but was not pierced by a single stake.

ARMY-BOUND

The army recruiter sent me to downtown Cleveland, Ohio, to take entrance tests. All expenses were to be paid. I only had two dollars on me when the recruiter gave me a bus ticket to Cleveland. I asked, "Where do I get off?" The recruiter replied, "At the bus station in Cleveland." At the first bus station in Cleveland, I got off; however, this station was on East Euclid around 70th Street. Well, with only two dollars, no taxi would give me a lift. This was in 1964 when Cleveland was having racial problems. Anyone that knows Cleveland, Ohio, knows you didn't want to be on the East Side then with all the dudes standing around swinging chains. Yep, you guessed it, I ran 70 blocks to the Manger Hotel, downtown. The darker it got, the faster I ran. I sure slept well that night.

I passed the test and was convinced to join the Army Security Agency and took my basic training at Fort Dix, New Jersey.

While standing in the chow line one day, a smart ass 2nd Lieutenant. approached me and started asking me where I was from. He happened to be a person I used to play football with when I was about 12 years old, 6 years earlier. Steve turned out to be my Company Commander.

During my stay at Fort Dix, Steve did not show any obvious favors.

However, I was one point from firing expert with the M-14; when the scores were posted, I had gained one point.

He watched out for me in little ways like assigning details to clean out the refrigerators at the firing range on super cold days, just keeping me out of the elements.

The next stop was Fort Gordon, Georgia, Signal Corp. By this time I had a Top Secret Crypto Clearance. Our barracks did not have a furnace that worked; all windows had to be open 12 inches due to spinal meningitis. The winter at Fort Gordon, Georgia, was the coldest I have ever been.

Next came Rothwesten, Germany - Assigned 319th US Army Security Agency Battalion. It was here near Kassle, Germany that I was talked into applying for flight school. I was told the Army would pay T.D.Y. (temporary duty status) extra money plus travel expense, to go to Frankfurt and take the tests for flight school.

I really wasn't interested in flying a helicopter. I probably hadn't seen 10 helicopters in my life but T.D.Y and travel pay made it worth taking all the tests. One day I was advised to go in front of a review board concerning flight school.

The next morning I put my uniform on and drove about two hours to be questioned by a Colonel, Major, and two Lieutenants. After 15 or 20 minutes of questions, the Colonel said, "Soldier, if we recommend your approval for flight school, would you make the army a career?" My reply was, "Sir for me to make the service a career, I would have to start out as a full bird Colonel like you."

Thirty days later, I left Germany and was sent to Fort Meade, Maryland. There I was oriented and briefed into the National Security Agency. This was in 1967; and after a few weeks, I was where I didn't want to be. So I went to personnel and asked what my status was on flight school. I was to report to flight school at Ft. Wolters, Texas, the following week.

Upon debriefing, the National Security Agency entered a letter into my 201 file which restricted my traveling outside the U.S.A. for 5 years without permission.

COMMENTARY:
A NEWSMAN'S OPINION

"The thing is, helicopters are different from planes. An airplane by its nature wants to fly, and if not interfered with too strongly by unusual events or by a deliberately incompetent pilot, it will fly.

A helicopter does not want to fly. It is maintained in the air by a variety of forces and controls working in opposition to each other; and if there is any disturbance in the delicate balance, the helicopter stops flying immediately and disastrously. There is no such thing as a gliding helicopter.

This is why being a helicopter pilot is so different from being an airplane pilot, and why, in general, airplane pilots are open, clear-eyed, buoyant extroverts, and helicopter pilots are brooders, introspective anticipators of trouble. They know if anything bad has not happened, it is about to."

Harry Reasoner

SOLO DAY

Confined Area Operations, Texas

My flight partner, J. Sult, and I had an I.P. (Instructor Pilot) by the name of J. Lewis, who was a very conscientious and cautious person. Sult and I must not have been the greatest of students because we were some of the last to solo in our flight class. However, the day came and

11

Lewis gave us our instructions on how the helicopter (TH-55) would act when he exited the helicopter because he weighed 200 pounds.

It was Sult's turn to fly, so he was going to solo first. The instructor and Sult landed in the grass between the lanes at the stage field. That is where they would park when a student was going to solo for the first time. I think maybe Lewis, the I.P., over-instructed the part about the weight change when he got out of the aircraft, because Sult smoothly picked up that helicopter and rolled it over right there.

Now, you have to understand it was the student's responsibility to sign off every flight. I ran over to the helicopter after it stopped flopping around to check on Sult's condition. He was already out of the aircraft filling out the logbook: Flt. 1 crashed J. Sult.

Well, needless to say, this shook up our instructor quite a bit; so I did not get to solo for another week.

Sult and I still were not the last to solo. We had a student everybody called "Dangerous Dan S." He was the last one, as I recall, taking the trip around the traffic pattern. He did really well until it came time to stop and land. His instructor had to run up in the tower and talk him down. Imagine that.

About 8 years later, I was on the Santa Monica Pier in California and guess who came walking by. Yep, Sult. He was now one of L.A.'s finest police officers.

Now, looking back at all the pilots that were killed in Vietnam, a lot of it came from complacence. The first sucking chest wound I ever witnessed was a result of a short time CH-47 pilot who was not wearing his chest protector.

A sniper shot him while he was in flight right through the center of the chest. "God does not always Protect the Ignorant."

ADF NIGHT CROSS-COUNTRY

Flight school night cross-country I was in a Huey (UH-1) with my flight partner Talbot. This night we were flying using our ADF (directional finding radio) for homing to our checkpoints. Everything went well on Talbot's flight and we were making our checkpoints just fine. Unfortunately, when it was my turn to fly, for some reason or another, Talbot was having a difficult time tuning the radio.

Out of frustration, I took my hand off the collective (control lever for maintaining pitch in the main rotor blades to keep a constant altitude) and started flying left-handed so I could tune the radio.

At this point, I should have let Talbot fly the aircraft. I guess I just did not think it would be a problem. During the time I was adjusting the radio, the helicopter started a slow descent. At 2500 feet, I looked outside and at 80 knots I was already below the tree line. I pulled back and made a cyclic climb and it was really close clearing the trees.

If I had screwed around with that radio a few seconds longer, we would have hit the ground going 80 knots and I do not think anybody would have ever figured out what happened.

SURVIVAL TRAINING

As in all military branches one must take a survival course before you can complete flight school. We were at Fort Rucker, Alabama; we were not fed all day because they wanted us hungry so we would have to provide for ourselves.

Oh, yes, they did have rattlesnake and grasshoppers, but that really wasn't very filling. Later in the afternoon after the classroom survival training it was time to start the real deal.

They loaded the entire flight class up in several deuces and a half (two and one-half ton trucks) and dropped us off in groups at different locations. Our mission was to build a fire, clean and cook a chicken, potatoes, and carrots. After doing this we were given coordinates, which were pick-up points.

If you missed the pick-up you would have to go farther, to another pick-up point, and all these points had time limits. They would truck you back to the barracks and if you were not one of the lucky, then you had to move on hoping to make the next check point in time and so on.
I was with a group of real men. I thought.

They really talked a good game. Big deer hunters, the kind of people you would actually want on your side in a difficult situation. This outing soon turned into a real nightmare. First of all, we could not get the fire hot enough to cook the chicken so we ended up trying to eat raw chicken, raw potatoes, and carrots.

After this, they gave us the signal to start for our pick-up point. By the way, they did have teams out also trying to capture us. Several guys did get captured and mildly tortured; such as blind folding, putting them in metal wall lockers, and yanking them up and down in a tree, or just spinning them around.

I really do not remember what happened, but I got separated from the group. Somehow, I ended up going with another group. Imagine this, south Alabama, so dark you cannot see your hand in front of your face, plus all those creatures that hang around the swamps. Anyway, what I am leading up to is the event where we came up on this road.

The road was made of white sand and as dark as it was you could see it was only five or six feet down to it. But, can you imagine how I felt when I jumped off the embankment.

I fell and I just kept falling until I went thru a tree and I grabbed hold of something and held on. That limb

17

was just long enough to break my fall as I landed flat on my back.

With that white sand, my depth perception was a little off. Instead of five to six feet down, it was more like twenty five to thirty feet down. WOW!

My new group and I made it to the next checkpoint without being captured and they gave us a lift back to the barracks. Oh yes, my old group was found the next morning by helicopter all standing around a fire--LOST.

FIRST NIGHT IN VIETNAM

As I mentioned when I left the National Security Agency they inserted a letter into my 201 files restricting my travel for five years. After flight school I got orders like all the rest of the pilots to go to Vietnam.

I was a little shocked about the orders because in my mind I was not in any way, shape or form expecting to go across the Pacific Ocean to Vietnam. I went to personnel and talked with the Colonel and explained about the letter in my 201 files.

He looked at my file and found the letter and said, "as long as this letter is in your file you cannot go to Vietnam." That was a good sound but before I could take another heartbeat, he took the letter out of the file, wadded it up, and threw it into the trashcan. Then he said, "Now, I see no reason why you cannot go to Vietnam."

My friend Robert and I had orders that specified that we were to be assigned to the 12th Aviation Group in Bien Hoa. Now, not thinking I was going to Vietnam I really did not pay a lot of attention to what aviation groups had the best duty.

19

Finally we were on approach to Long Bien and we were picked up and escorted by two Cobra gunships to the landing threshold.

After unloading and getting settled we finally got assigned our sleeping arrangements. Robert was on the bottom bunk and I was on the top one and both of us were happy to be assigned to the 12th Aviation Group.

However, at 3:00 a.m. we were awakened abruptly and informed to get our things together because we were being reassigned to the First Air Cavalry and the plane was leaving for An Khe (Kay) in a few minutes.

Upon hearing this, Robert broke down and started crying. Of course, being ignorant of the outfits in Vietnam, I had no idea what was ahead. I asked Robert what was wrong. He replied, "Pilots that go to the 1st Air Cavalry normally do not return home."

When we arrived in An Khe I was assigned to Headquarters Company of the 2nd Brigade. As soon as I went to my new company and met a few of the personnel, I was told that, as of this date, no pilot had returned home in over two years without injury. I knew right then that conditions or flying techniques had to change.

A Few Days After Arrival In Vietnam

ED FISHER, An Old Friend

I was at An Khe being processed a few days before I went to my unit in the field. I was walking across the base and three young soldiers saluted me, so I returned the salute. After about three or four steps I realized I knew one of them. I turned, he turned, and we called each other by name. It was Ed Fisher, a good friend with whom I had gone to school in Newton Falls, Ohio. We even played on the same little league baseball team. Seeing someone I knew, well, it was a joyous moment.

While I was in the hospital being treated for mortar wounds, Ed had gotten shot in his shoulder and was sent home. I didn't see Ed again. He became a schoolteacher and was killed in a car crash a few years later.

WOUNDED IN ACTION

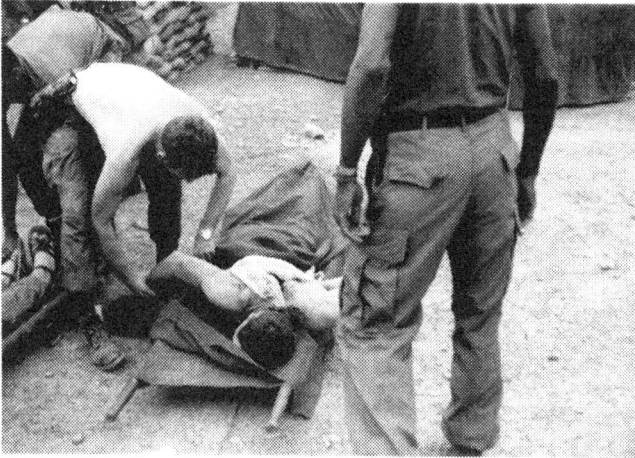

After Mortar Attack

It was April 8, 1968, LZ (loading zone) Jane about 4:00 a.m. If you have never heard incoming mortars, it is really a sound and an adrenalin rush that would be hard to explain. It is a loud whistle followed by a big boom, light flashes and the piercing whistling sounds of shrapnel.

After a few of the pilots went home we started reconditioning a large bunker so a couple of us new guys could use it. We had the roof off. We were going to reinforce the roof so we could add more sandbags.

23

During the construction period we were sleeping in a tent (GP Med) with little or no overhead coverage.

It happened; a mortar attack and the 1st round hit right above my head and was detonated by impacting the tent. All I heard was the whistle, boom, flash, and it felt like someone hit me in the back with a 2X4 board. I yelled, "I'm hit!" Then two others, Lee and John, yelled out also.

At this time, we ran into the roofless bunker. The bunker was about 10' X 10' and 8' deep. I remember the three of us kind of huddled up in a corner looking up into the night with mortars still coming. I can remember as clear as if it were yesterday.

That roofless bunker was as large as a football field, because we knew the next mortar would fall in with us. Finally it was over.

The medics arrived and started checking us out. John and Lee were only hit once or twice apiece so they were in good shape. I, on the other hand, had put an ammo box (wood) at the head of my cot. That's right, not only did I have metal shrapnel in me but the wooden box was shredded.

The medics counted 134 holes on my upper back. I guess they were entertaining me while waiting for the med-e-vac (medical evacuation). By the way, I cannot ever remember sleeping on my stomach since that night.

Bloody Hat That Was Under The Cot

The helicopter came around 7:00 a.m. and I was med-e-vaced to a field hospital about 10 miles away in Quang Tri (tree).

After being prepped for surgery, I was rolled into this insulated tent and put on a gurney that was so cold I think I stuck to it.

The surgeons came into the room wearing overcoats. They told me it was to help cut down on germs. Then the doctor said, "Try to count from 10 backwards to 1". All I remember was 10-9-8-77777777. That sodium pentothal was some great drug. It was known as the "truth" serum.

I remember waking up and the doctor asking me questions. He said," Jim, do you take your malaria pill?" I said, "No". At this point I came out of it because his next question was, "Jim, how about the daily malaria pill?" I was awake so I responded, yes. I lied.

The next day or so, I was put on a C-130 airplane and flown to Qui Nhon (kwee nyoung). The doctors, in Vietnam, realized that postoperatively they should not immediately stitch up some wounds. Instead, after the incision there's drainage for five days to help prevent infections and allow healing from the inside.

Well, during this 1 1/2 hour flight my bandages were more wet than they were dry and stuck to my wounds. The surgeons took out the large pieces of metal, but left the small stuff because it would do more damage digging than leaving it alone.

When we arrived in Qui Nhon, everyone that was on stretchers was placed on rails like an assembly line; then started the triage procedures.

When my turn came, this cute little nurse came over and said, "I am gonna make you tough." She proceeded to rip the bandages off my back. Woo, I could feel the wounds popping open because everything was dried and stuck together.

I turned to express my displeasure when I saw her face. I thought she was going to lose it right there. However, that was one nurse that treated me very well for the rest of my stay at Qui Nhon.

After 5 days, I was finally given that great drug again and they finished stitching me up. I stayed for another few days and then was transported to Cam Ranh (Ron) Bay for convalescence. Cam Ranh Bay was beautiful. The beaches were nice, the water clean, and sea turtles and large lizards were in abundance.

Because I was raised most of my life in the mid-west, I never had a problem getting sunburned. Ha! Let me tell you, I got so burned, I could not even bend my feet to walk. A full bird doctor stopped me, and told me everything he could to humiliate me short of an article 15, (disciplinary action) because of my severe burn. He was pissed.

Anyway, the stitches came out and it was time for physical therapy. I had the meanest female major that I ever came across. This lady stayed on me constantly. By the time I was ready to leave, those beautiful scars that were barely noticeable had stretched to three fourths to an inch wide. Well it was time to be released and return to my unit.

GLASS-EATER

Cam Ranh Bay Rehab

My stay in Cam Ranh Bay was for more than a month, so I had an opportunity to observe some strange events. Movies were shown outside, and we had an officer's club. One evening after everyone had a few drinks and were feeling their oats, the officers started telling each other who was in the best outfit.

I sat there thinking nothing good can come out of this. One of the officers that got into the verbal match was an ex-cop from Chicago, who was airborne trained, and the other was a member of the Rangers.

Now these two guys sat there yelling, "AIRBORNE"! "RANGER"! This kept on going for about ten minutes until finally the ex-cop from Chicago reached over to the bar and picked up a glass. He then took a bite out of the glass, chewed it up, and swallowed it.

He then handed the remaining portion of the glass to the other officer as he said, "AIRBORNE!" There came a hush over the entire club while waiting for the ranger to reply. He did not. I guess it was just tougher to be Airborne, rather than a Ranger.

CLEVE, THE ROOSTER

Most of the time in Vietnam, when you needed to get somewhere, you just asked around until you found a helicopter or jeep heading where you were going. I was trying to hitch a ride back to LZ Jane (loading zone at my home base) after I was released from the hospital and I ran into a soldier that was on his way home.

He asked me if I would take his pet rooster. I asked, "Where is he?" and he replied, "In my pocket." The rooster had been in his pocket so long that all the feathers were worn off. It was a pitiful looking creature. Anyway, I took the rooster and I named him after our red-headed executive officer, Cleveland. I just called him Cleve.

Now Cleve loved to eat insects, grasshoppers, etc. And he liked to roost on the C.O.'s chair (Commanding Officer) and would crap on it quite often. You could hear the C.O. chasing him out of the tent. I was, as far as I knew, the only pilot that did not drink, so I was in bed usually early.

This night, around 9:30, everybody ousted me out of bed to show me something. Right before my very eyes Cleve could not stand up. His legs were just like rubber. It seems they were injecting Cleve with vodka. They gave him another shot, he laid on his back, did a 360 degree turn, kicked his legs up and they fell like lead.

That was the end of Cleve the Rooster. The way he passed on reminded me of a cartoon character.

TAIL ROTOR FAILURE

As I mentioned before, helicopter pilot slots were hard to keep filled. When I got orientated a little by flying co-pilot in Hueys on command and control missions, I was ready to transition into the aircraft they used for scout missions, the OH-13 or Bell 47. We had to have five hours of flight time to be considered checked out in the OH-13. Most helicopter pilots went to Vietnam with around 250 hours of total flight time, which was just enough time to be dangerous. I believe that at about the 400-500 hour level is when I really felt the feeling of flying by touch and getting away from doing everything mechanical.

My first mission was to carry something to LZ Evans (loading zone) located about 15 minutes to the south of LZ Jane. I got in the aircraft, started it up, and all this time I had a 30 mph tail wind blowing up the revetment (sandbags stacked up about five feet high on the front and both sides of the helicopter for protection).

As I went thru the run-up procedure and got the aircraft light on the skids and was pulling collective (pitch in the blades), I came up and a gust of wind caused me to yaw (nose of helicopter swivels from one side to the other). At the time, I did not know that the tail rotor had hit the sandbags and popped out the short shaft that comes from the transmission and drives the tail rotor. I continued to back out of the revetment and started to turn when all of a sudden, the helicopter started to spin. In flight school when the aircraft started spinning you were taught to chop or close the throttle eliminating torque and the helicopter would stop spinning and then you could finish the procedure with a hovering auto-rotation. Not me, being the ace I was, I kinda panicked and just bottomed the collective.

At least, I hit the ground level and did not do anymore damage to the aircraft. However, if I had not backed out of the revetment when I did, it would have started spinning in the revetment. These revetments only had a few feet of clearance on each side so I am sure it would have been a catastrophe. "GPTIS"

AK 47--OUT OF WINDOW

I was sent up to Khe Sanh (Kay Shun), or close to there, to drop off a crypto officer so he could repair some equipment.

He remained there, so I leisurely flew back at about 50 feet. It was just another routine flight as I went down Hwy 1, which I think was the road through Quang Tri. Suddenly, I saw an AK-47 come out of a window; I was helpless, so I lowered the nose to pick up speed.

As I approached the gun, I was in a slight dive; from 50 feet you cannot dive for too long. Instead of leading me a little, the Viet Cong waited until I was abeam his location. RIP! That was all I heard. Then I saw the commo (communication) wire strung across the road, which wrapped around my mast and control rods. I did not take a round, but I did have to land and find a pair of pliers to cut the commo wire off. "God really does Protect the Ignorant."

LIEUTENANT ABBOT

At Dong Ha in 1968, a Lt. Abbot and I were assisting the First Cavalry who was aiding the marines north of the city. The lieutenant and I were on the ground waiting for our mission to come in.

After being briefed and told what we were supposed to do, we headed to our aircrafts, OH-13 S models. Lt. Abbot was the team leader: Silver 11 & 12 were our call signs. Just as we started to enter the helicopters, a crew chief came running up with a letter for Lt. Abbott.

Abbott looked at me and said, "Jim, this is a letter from my sister. Let me read it. I might never get another chance."

Ten minutes later we were climbing out of Dong Ha. We almost always flew low level. As we climbed thru 1,000 feet, the lieutenant took a direct hit from a B-40 rocket and he just disappeared.

VIEW OF THE DMZ

During the monsoon season on another one of these milk-run missions, I was sent to drop off a passenger in a Bell 47-OH-13 S up near the DMZ (Demiliterized Zone). Flying up there was no problem, but on my return flight it started raining. It rained so hard during this season (the monsoons) that the only way to see was to fly sideways. With no doors and flying sideways, it was a slow flight back. Of course, the magnetic compass did not work, so I was flying by the seat of my pants when I realized I was crossing a large river.

Now, I did not cross the river coming up, so I was not going to cross it going back to LZ Jane. I made a course correction and finally found landmarks I recognized and flew back to my base. Later, I found out that that river was the DMZ and it separated North and South Vietnam.

DROPPED GRENADE

As you probably have heard, there were a tremendous number of people killed by pilot error. There were many incidents of bad judgment; I should not be here today. However, you must, "learn from your mistakes and the mistakes of other's because you won't live long enough to make all the mistakes yourself."

We had a few rules on the helicopter but one was: anytime the door-gunner pulled a pin on any type of grenade, he was to pull the pin outside the aircraft, he was to hold it outside until it was dropped. We kept 2 or 3 boxes of several types of grenades: frag, smoke, and white phosphorous.

The white phosphorous grenades worked on the principle that after they exploded, the particles that came apart and were exposed to the air would burn until they burned themselves out or one somehow cut off the oxygen supply to it.

This incident was hearsay because if you didn't see it, you don't know how much of the story was true. While I was in the hospital, right after the fighting in Khe Sanh, the 3rd brigade went into the A Shau Valley. This is where I was told that a friend of ours from their scout team had this incident. They were using a white phosphorous grenade and the door-gunner dropped it inside the cockpit. Imagine knowing you're going to blow up and there's nothing you can do about it.

SPIDER WEB

We occasionally would get some goofy missions. For example, "How about hovering over that tree and tell me where that sniper fire is coming from."

The one I think about an awful lot was when we were called out to help a platoon that was pinned down by enemy fire. This was my own stupidity by not getting a better location on the friendlies. Also as I look back, the Cobra Gunships should have been called and not the scout team with only 2 door-gunners with M60 machine guns and 2 skid-mounted M-60s. It turned out that the enemy was between the friendlies and us.

Not knowing this, which was my fault (complacency), I led my team down the tree line where the North Vietnamese Army was dug in. Needless to say, they opened up on the 2 OH-13s (Bell 47s). We realized we were where we did not want to be. So I said, "break left" because if we got shot down we would be over our own troops. This is one of many events I relive. When we turned left, I don't know how many machine guns were in that tree line but with one tracer in every five rounds, it looked like we were flying into a red and green spider web. It's hard to believe that with all those bullets, neither aircraft took a hit. We

39

pulled back and called in the 2nd of the 20th Cavalry "BLUE MAX" who were our cobra gunship backups; they cleaned up the mess. "GPTIS"

SHELLED BY FRIENDLIES

We were still at LZ Jane, which is in the northern sector of South Vietnam near Quang Tri (tree). The 3rd Brigade of the Marines was in Dang Ha just north of Quang Tri. I do not remember the date. I had experienced many mortar attacks but never had I experienced incoming artillery rounds. It was late, around 1 a.m., and everybody that was not on duty was in their bunker.

This was a good thing because, when those artillery rounds started coming in with such a screaming sound before impact, words cannot describe it.

After the initial explosions, the shells blew apart and all the pieces you could hear whistling in all directions. It probably was the most awesome, helpless sound I have heard in my life. Finally, someone got in touch with the Marines and got a cease-fire.

I think only three or four of our aircraft were damaged. It could have been a lot worse if it had happened at a different time of day.

STUCK PEDALS

We had just returned from a scout mission, where the door-gunner had shot a lot of M60 machine gun rounds. Before I could get shut down, my commanding officer came up to the aircraft and asked if I would take a passenger to Quang Tri for an emergency conference. All I had to do was drop him off and return. However, due to all those shell casings left from the scout mission and the vibrations of the helicopter, some of the brass had fallen into and locked the pedal controls.

The pedals control the tail rotor; the tail rotor is a necessity during power changes and landings. The emergency procedure for this incident is a running landing. So going through my mind was, where will be the best place to accomplish this! After thinking about the situation and knowing the POL (refueling point) was on the side of a hill, I descended to the height of the hill. I did a running landing on the top, stopped, got out and removed the brass from the pedals. I refueled and returned to the flight line just like nothing happened. Just another day.

WAYNE N.

Wayne was a tall black gentleman that was a pilot in the 2nd Brigade of the First Cavalry. I think he was already there when I arrived, but I am not sure. He flew command and control missions. Some of his incidents happened while I was in the hospital, so this is hearsay. The story goes that Wayne flew a brand new H-Model Huey into Khe Sanh and parked it in a revetment.

While he and the crew were standing around and waiting, he saw, a few revetments away, a flight school classmate. So Wayne and the crew went over to chat. Just as they arrived at the other revetment, they heard an awful noise; it was a 122 mm. rocket and it hit Wayne's new Huey with a direct hit.

Anyway, time goes by and I get back from the hospital and start flying scouts. I did not and don't consider myself as an elite scout pilot like the rest, I just wanted to survive. Wayne would bug us all the time to let him go on a mission with us. So, one evening we decided not to get into much trouble, and we took Wayne with us. I was flying the #2 bird that day and Hughes was Silver–one-one (11).

After we got clear of the LZ., Hughes told Wayne to test the M60 machine gun. He was having a blast of fun.

Then I heard "grenade out"; I was watching them and drifting away at the same time. Then the door-gunner said, "look out" and right in front of us was a single pole in a rice patty about 50 feet high. Now, I was only 15 feet above the ground and, to this day, I don't know how I was able to put that helicopter in an attitude to get around that pole going 70 knots, but I did. Thank you, LORD.

At this time, we were about halfway through our mission and Wayne had shot the M60 machine gun and dropped grenades. He just couldn't let that be enough when he saw the M-79 grenade launcher.

Hughes gave him very clear instructions that the helicopter would travel as fast as the round from the grenade launcher, so be sure to shoot it away from the aircraft. Wayne did just that, away from the helicopter, to the front! Oh boy, they flew right into the same area where the grenade went off and with all that shrapnel, luckily they only took one hit. It just happened to be in Wayne's neck. Wayne said, "I'm hit, I'm bleeding, what should I do?" Hughes said, "Well if I were you, I'd hold my neck and put pressure on it so I wouldn't bleed to death."

Wayne made it all right, but he was the only person I knew or heard about shooting himself with a grenade launcher in Vietnam and receiving a purple heart for it!

ATHEIST--not

As everyone knows, it's hard to find an atheist in a foxhole. I have not known a helicopter pilot in my lifetime that admitted to being one. When I was leaving for Vietnam my father told me, "Son, I was in World War II and was in 8 major battles and I came home. Son, you will not come back." Now, this was the most brilliant or moronic thing the old man ever said to me.

Now, imagine every day thinking back on what dear old Dad said. This motivated me to the max because I was going to show him. Every morning we got up just before daylight, so we could do a first-light reconnaissance and make sure the enemy hadn't moved in on us during the night. However, before I got out of my cot I would say a prayer, "Dear God, please allow me to return to this cot tonight." Before I fell asleep I would always tell God: "thanks" for my safe return.

Many times you would hear on the radio when someone got in trouble they would say "oh my God" and this made me believe that there were no atheist helicopter pilots.

RAT--big one

You probably have heard tales about the rats in Vietnam being as large as cats; let me tell you those are not tales. If you don't believe me, ask Warrant Officer Berry. We were asleep one night at LZ Jane in our bunker. Our beds were wooden stands, on which we would lay air mattresses and enclose them with mosquito nets. Now imagine being inside this hole about 8 feet deep and 10 feet square with only one way in and out.

WO Berry was awakened and started screaming. It appeared that this cat-size rat was inside his mosquito net and had his big toe in its front paws and was eating his toe. The rat got away, but Berry had to take rabies shots around his belly button and I can remember he couldn't fasten his belt for a while. Now, we were already short of pilots. Oh well, I guess there are people that would do anything to get out of work.

LARUE SIN JOY

The French were in Vietnam for many years before the Americans got involved. There was a road in the northeast of the country the French called "the street without joy." I was told they lost ten-thousand lives on this road because it was so narrow, impossible to turn around on and had rice patties on both sides. It was great for ambushes.

The 1st Cavalry made this area, close to the DMZ, a free-fire zone. This meant that any military-age males were to be shot. I was really not as gung-ho as most of my counterparts mainly because I was more concerned about self-preservation. Most of the younger scout pilots were very aggressive and got a rush from their missions.

Our mission, as the Silver Team, on the last-light reconnaissance was this area near the DMZ. As we went up " the street without joy" close to the DMZ, we noticed a rice patty with 11 or 12 military-age males harvesting rice. My #2 team partner was all excited and wanted to shoot them. It seemed very strange to me that there were so many of them together, so I told everyone to hold their fire and not to act suspicious. We went back to base and made a report with S2 and told them about the situation.

47

The next morning the 2nd of the 5th First Cavalry Mechanized Infantry unit surrounded this small village that was very close to the beach. As the tanks moved in, soldiers came out of bunkers with anti-tank weapons and started blowing away the tanks. The tanks pulled back and called in the Air Force to do a little bombing. Ha--five days later-- the Air Force finally softened the area enough so the tanks and infantry could go in. It turned out that those bunkers were cement and the head count after the Air Force finished was around 5,000 North Vietnam Army personnel. It turned out to be an R&R retreat for the North Viet Army.

To this day, I cannot think of anything good that could have happened if we had fired at the soldiers in the rice patties. I'm sure there were a lot of machine guns in the tree lines just waiting for us to do something stupid.

Sometimes you have got to listen to your gut feelings. Again, I did feel protected this day.

DOCTOR--North Vietnamese

We were on a mission with the ground troops. As they would search an area, we would be overhead to make sure no one ran out the back. As we continued to circle, I noticed a person that was well-dressed and clean-looking. As I continued watching him he became paranoid and was doing things that seemed abnormal. I called the troops on the ground and pointed him out so they could do a better check on him.

A week later 2 AK-44s still in cosmoline (shipping grease) were delivered to me by an officer. He said it was in appreciation for assisting them on their mission. Not only did they find a weapon cache but, also, that individual turned out to be a doctor in the North Vietnamese Army with the rank of Colonel. His job was to go from village to village taking care of the wounded Viet Cong and North Vietnam Army. He was just making his routine rounds when he got captured.

49

MOUNTAINTOP

I really had a difficult time trying to put a name on this event. I was the only pilot in my unit that did not drink. I was the Sunday Morning Designated Person to fly the chaplain from LZ to LZ so he could deliver the Word.

In twelve months, I flew three different chaplains. The first was an ex-FBI Agent who loved throwing CS grenades (tear gas) at kids who threw rocks at us as we were flying by.

The second was called "The Jumping Chaplain." I was told he would parachute into the troops when he was in Korea. The third chaplain was young and this was one of our experiences together.

The chaplain always carried a bag with a strap long enough to hang on his shoulder for carrying convenience. Our first stop on a nice and bright Sunday morning was a ridgeline high in the mountains. The ground troops had taken chainsaws and cleared this area enough for a helicopter to land. However, most people do not consider slopes or the angle of the terrain when preparing for a helicopter landing.

This ridgeline was a finger of land off the main mountain and was sloping away at probably 15 degrees or greater. The Bell 47 I was flying was used for training so it had duel controls. After circling and figuring out the winds and the best approach route, I started my descent. At this altitude the winds are usually strong and it's necessary to take advantage of them the best and safest way possible. When I got closer to the LZ (landing zone) I realized it was on the top and edge of a steep cliff. As I continued I also noticed the angle of the slope and determined it was too steep to land. So I told the chaplain that I intended to put the skid on my side against the slope and hold it so he could climb out.

At about 3 feet above the ground, with my pucker factor ultra high, I was concentrating on the slope and getting prepared to put the skid on the slope. The next thing I realized, the helicopter was going out of control. The ground troops were all running trying to take cover. Then I suddenly realized what happened. The chaplain had jumped out at about three feet, changing the center of gravity without letting me know. What made it worse was the chaplain standing by the helicopter with the strap on his bag wrapped around the cyclic (control used to terminate an approach and stop at a hover). He was yanking and pulling trying to get it loose. Meanwhile, here I am trying to regain control, but by this time my RPM was so low that I knew it was all over for me.

All of a sudden, a gust of wind blew me off the cliff. Here I am falling vertical, looking straight up and then I heard myself say, "Jim, you got to do something or you're gonna die." By this time the RPM was so low, as was my experience level, but I did all I could. I opened the throttle all the way and started to pump the collective up and down, changing pitch and trying to build RPM. Finally, I was able to get in a horizontal attitude. Just as I was starting to fall into the treetops, the helicopter started to shake and shutter and finally started to build RPM and fly. I recovered and flew back to base. Within 20 minutes I started an out-of-control body shake and I remained in this condition for over 4 hours!

There is not a day that passes that I don't think of this event. Because with my experience level today, I know that it is impossible to put a Bell 47 into those attitudes with low RPM and have enough power to recover in the short amount of time I had to react. "GOD REALLY DOES PROTECT THE IGNORANT, SOMETIMES." This was one of those "sometimes." By the way, the chaplain gave me two bottles of communion wine and said he was just trying to help out.

DAY OFF

After flying one month and logging 130 hours, I was given a day off. So, I flew an OH-13 Bell 47 to Wonder Beach where there was a lot of security. It was the port where all the rations were brought in from the ships. Anyway, I blew up my air mattress and started floating on the ocean next to the shore. There was a huge supply ship anchored there. Well, I fell asleep on the mattress and drifted. Several hours later, I woke up shocked and panicked, and didn't know where I was. Finally, I recognized the ship, which was only about 1/2 inch on the horizon. I was so far out I could not take the chance of going ashore and walking back. So, I paddled probably 4 hours non-stop back to shore. What would I have done if I had not awakened, when I did, and could not have seen the ship in the distance? I did sleep well that night.

WONDER BEACH

It seems that a motivated person with the intentions of helping others always finds friends to help out. I don't even remember how this friendship began. An N.C.O. (non-commissioned officer) by the name of Tomlin was in charge of Wonder Beach. I don't know how it got its name. It was where supplies were unloaded, mainly food, from huge ships that would anchor offshore.

The supplies would be unloaded and transported by an amphibious boat called a duck. After the supplies came ashore, they were put in huge walk-in refrigeration units that were called reefers. SSG (Staff Sergeant) Tomlin approached me with an offer that I thought I couldn't turn down with approval by the commander.

Tomlin had a brother stationed in Da Nang which was 1-2 hours of flight time away. He said, "Jim, if you take me to see my brother, I will keep you supplied with steaks, chicken and anything else I have that you want."

After I took SSG Tomlin to Da Nang to see his brother, everything for our flight at H.Q. Co. 2nd Brigade of the 1st Cavalry got better. We had steak, chicken and many other items that we would not have gotten, if it hadn't been for this arrangement. After this, the commander made me the official procurer for the flight.

ICE DEAL

Where we were located there was no ice. In fact, we drank warm orange kool-aid often un-sweetened because that's all we had besides warm water.

My mind was always trying to figure out ways to make life better for everyone, and ice was a problem. One day I approached Tomlin and asked if those reefers would make ice. He said, "Yes, but it might take a few days." So that's when it hit me, we could make our own ice. I went to the mess tent and scrounged around until I found 30 number 10 cans. I got in the helicopter (Bell 47) that the commander allowed me to use and I took those cans to Wonder Beach.

Upon my arrival, I filled the cans with water and put 10 cans in 3 reefers each. Now, in 3 days I went back and they were frozen hard. From that day on, until Tomlin's outfit moved out, I rotated 10 cans every day, and my flight had plenty of ice every evening.

When SSG Tomlin's outfit got ready to relocate, he said he would give me a truck and trailer filled with one-inch plywood sheets of mahogany but only if I would take him to Da Nang again to see his brother. I did. The trailer was an eighteen-wheeler type rig. My problem was what to do with it. I knew we were going to move to LZ Nancy soon, so that's where I headed.

ICE-CREAM RUN

After SSG.Tomlin moved on I would fly by Wonder Beach just to check it out. One day I was coming from Da Nang after a heavy rain and decided to go by the beach. To my surprise the little area was totally flooded, except where everyone lived. I stopped and asked, "Hey, is there anything I can do for you guys?" The reply was, "If you will go to LZ Sharon and bring us our mail, we will give you all the ice cream we have." I really was doing them a favor fetching their mail because I knew how important mail was. What I didn't know was these guys were running an ice cream factory. Wow -- they gave me 98 gallons of chocolate ice cream. Now imagine, it is 100 degrees, and I have 98 gallons of ice cream to fly back to the base. It took 20 minutes. We had no idea what a helicopter would look like covered with melting ice cream. Ha!--totally, entirely covered with chocolate. Everyone thought we had a hydraulic failure.

BEER-RUN

I did most of the wheeling and dealing for the Headquarters Flight of the 2nd Brigade of the First Cavalry. This day I was to fly a milk-run to Da Nang and buy beer and soda from the PX. (Post Exchange) One thing we just did not figure very often in Vietnam was weight and balance.

It was hot and humid and the density altitude did not always favor helicopters. My crew and I loaded the chopper down with beer and soda to such a degree that I could not hover. This was really stupid. I picked up the Huey H-1 and sort of dove it off an embankment hoping to get translational lift before I hit the other side of the bank. HE protected me again and just before the main rotor hit the bank (2-3ft) the aircraft shook and vibrated and we flew away. It was a beautiful ride home north along the coastline.

WEIRD HAROLD

I met this Med-E-Vac pilot while I was in the hospital. I had no idea he stayed at the end of the flight line at LZ Jane. I would go to visit this pilot and he had a friend, another pilot, by the name of Harold Hicks.

I think Harold had a degree in math or something like that. Anyway, he was always hounding me to let him be my door-gunner. Finally, I had had enough and I told my backup that I was taking Harold and we were not going to look for trouble. This was a last-light reconnaissance, so we just went out to see if anything strange was happening. We came up on this free-fire zone and an old man in a sand pan was poling himself down the river. I looked at Harold and said, "This is a free-fire zone, and no one is supposed to be here; so take the M-60 machine gun and kill him."

I wished I had this on video, because Weird Harold took that machine gun and started firing. Four hundred rounds later, we were out of bullets and the little old man was still standing and moving that sand pan down the river.

Next, Harold started dropping grenades, about 20 or so total, in the old man's direction. Now you have to realize, I'm hovering about 50 feet over this old man's head

60

the whole time. Finally, I told Harold, "This is Papason's Day." So, we headed back to the base. Weird Harold was happy to have been a door-gunner for one mission.

Now that I know the damage it can do to you, I am glad he was a bad shot. A few days later, I went over to check on Harold. They said, "Haven't you heard? An officer came by to get Harold to sign a document."

It seems when everybody else signed an extension after flight school, Harold was absent and did not sign the form. It turned out he had been out of the service for 10 months, so I was told. Imagine all the excitement he would have missed if he had not gone to Vietnam on his own time.

FLAGPOLE--ooops!

Steve was a redhead and was as crazy as crazy could be. He was always laughing and joking around and this event probably would not have been so funny except the way Steve could justify it.

They were on a last-light reconnaissance scout mission and they played around too long and got caught by darkness. Anyway, on their way back to base and like I said, it was dark, and they were flying low-level across this village. Before they could realize or see what was happening someone started shooting at the scout team. Now, Steve, trying to avoid being shot down was making evasive maneuvers and encountered a flagpole. Since it was dark he had no idea what he hit but the engine was still making a noise and the helicopter was still flying so he flew by to base.

Upon arriving we all ran out to see what was happening. That flagpole had torn away the entire bubble on the Bell-47. It resembled one of those do-it-yourself kits. FORTUNATE

LZ NANCY (loading zone)

The Headquarters of the 2nd Brigade of the 1st Cavalry was moving from LZ Jane to LZ Nancy a few miles south. When there is a decision to move or relocate, several companies are sent ahead to set up and secure a perimeter.

An engineer outfit to make a flight line and roads follows. The first time I went to LZ Nancy was a few weeks after the perimeter was set up. The security had a back slide and the North Viet Army slipped inside the wire and started throwing shrapnel charges into the bunkers. Upon impact these would explode causing extreme concussion and blowing bodies apart.

There are many wild helicopter pilots and we called them "cowboys". This was how I thought of my pilot-in-command this day because he was going to demonstrate to me a hot approach. Now, this procedure is done by making a very fast approach with a steep flare-and-pitch pull at the bottom to stop the rate of closure. In doing this, you create a tremendous rotor wash that blows dust, and everything not tied down gets blown away. Sometimes people just do not make good decisions and this was one. He was demonstrating this approach into LZ Nancy the next morning.

63

After the LZ got overrun, they had all the dead bodies lying side-by-side covered with poncho liners. Yep, he blew the ponchos away and exposed bodies with heads, legs, and arms blown away from the bodies.

BURIED TRAILER

The next time I went to LZ Nancy was with the truck and trailer from Wonder Beach. When I arrived there I had no idea what I was going to do with it. As I was driving through the gate, I stopped and asked where the flight line was going to be so I could get an idea where to park. The guard pointed to a bulldozer and said that the runway was being prepared now.

I drove the truck and trailer over to the dozer operator and asked, "What would it take to get this trailer buried." The operator replied, "Man, I have not tasted a beer in over three months." AAH; I just felt some negotiations getting started so, I replied, "How big a hole can I get for two cases of Bud?" He grinned and said, "As big as you want." I did not tell you but this was a huge bulldozer. In fact, the blade was as wide or wider than I needed.

Within twenty minutes I was pulling the trailer in and disconnecting the truck. We put steel planks across the top of the trailer and covered it with several layers of sandbags. I left the 136 sheets of one inch, four by eight foot mahogany plywood and I hoped no one would cut my lock off and take them.

65

TOM HOWE

Crash and Death Site of Tom Howe

Tom was and still is one of the best men I have ever known. He was our maintenance officer and was very knowledgeable about his job. He also had a good history of military service. He started as an enlisted soldier, became a crew chief and eventually, was selected to be President Ike's crew chief on a H-34. He said that that aircraft had an autopilot, which made that helicopter ahead of its time. This was in the 1950s, so this made Tom around 40 years old compared to the rest of the pilots who all were under 25 years of age.

I think Tom had a big influence on the way I looked at difficult situations. He would always tell me to do my best and not to worry about the things I cannot change. It was Tom who helped me when I took the truck and trailer to LZ Nancy with all the plywood. He designed and helped to build our shack on the end of the trailer I had buried in the side of a hill.

Tom and I became roommates and we shared the trailer and shack. In the shack we put a sink and put two 55-gallon barrels on the roof. They were filled with water and one of them had a heater that worked by burning jet fuel, so we actually had hot and cold running water.

We also had some mahogany plywood left over, so we built a horse-shoe bar. Now this was making everybody jealous. By this time we had a new company commander and his rank was that of a major. Anyway, he came to Tom and me complaining about the situation with morality. So we decided to help the other pilots to build themselves some type of quarters.

We were able to scrap and trade for bundles of plywood and two-by-fours. When everything was said and done the pilots looked like they lived in a one-level hotel with a hall all the way down the middle of the building and rooms on both sides. Finally, everyone was happy. While we were out trading and dealing we came across a marine quartermaster in Quang Tri that had received eleven pool tables by mistake. They were supposed to go to Korea. Well one AK-47 bought us two pool tables for the shack; so now we had a game room. During the construction of the shack we installed screen louver windows with flaps on the outside for light control at night. The shack became a popular place so we planned a beer and soda run to Da Nang to purchase a refrigerator from the PX.

Shack, Sweet Shack

At the same time, I ran across a roommate of mine from flight school. He told me he was the motor pool officer here in Da Nang and explained his job to me including the items he had control of such as generators. I asked what would the possibility be of signing out a 5 KW generator. "No problem," he said. This was turning out to be a very successful beer and soda run. I was able to purchase a refrigerator and a generator to run it. Thank you, Jim Steele.

Now, with a refrigerator in the shack we had cold drinks for everybody and pool tables, and many a night we played extremely late.

For emergency situations, we had the trailer covered with steel planks (PSP) and layers of sandbags that could have taken a pretty hard hit. Also since the floor of the trailer was thick and set fairly high off the ground, we realized we could build a trapdoor leading under the trailer just in case of a mortar attack. We would just hit the door and we were under the trailer. This trailer was approximately 8-10 feet wide and 40 feet long so we had plenty of space.

Tom and I spent a lot of time together and grew very close. We were on another beer and soda run to Da Nang. On our return (we always followed the shoreline back north), we ran into some heavy rain. We thought if we could find a place to land we would. There it was an airstrip. We knew the enemy did not have anything like that so we landed. We were met by a bunch of Americans that had a contract to clean and drag Hue (whey) harbor to keep it ocean-going. We made friends and would stop in on occasion for a visit. It turned out they had an air conditioner repairman with whom I traded an AK-47 for a 28,000 BTU air conditioner. So now our trailer was capable of maintaining a cool 65 degrees--wow this was nice. However, in the 1st Cavalry, the only comfort we were allowed was a cot and sleeping bag.

Anyway, our relationship with that American construction company at Coca Beach across the bay from Hue became better and better. They lived in a mobile home community. They had a large barge with mobile homes stacked two or three high with a large dining room on the main floor and their food was exceptional. Tom and I found out that these 80 Americans had 40 Korean ladies to cook and clean for them. They invited Tom and me to come and spend a Sunday afternoon with them. It seemed like they had it good. Tom and I convinced the major this would be good public relations because these guys had supplies we could not get. So the major said we could go one Sunday after I flew the chaplain. Well, we made the date to go and Tom was to have the helicopter refueled and ready to go.

The chaplain and I were landing and I noticed a bunch of the crews coming to meet the helicopter. After I shut down and was clear of the rotor blades they approached me with the news. A few minutes before I landed Tom was at the refueling point, and he was lifting off in an (LOH) OH-6. The only thing I think could have happened involved the mini-guns we used that fired 2000-4000 rounds per minute and the vertical fin on the tail boom. If it had metal fatigue and broke off going into the tail rotor, it could cause the helicopter to invert. It appeared Tom had broken his neck. I never got back to Coco Beach or Hue again. I just kept thinking this must have been an omen, because if it had happened a few minutes later I would have been with him. I don't think that there is a day that passes without Tom entering my mind. I always wonder how his family made out.

COLONEL R. McKINNON

In the 1st Air Cavalry, the only comforts we were authorized to have was a sleeping bag, air mattress, and cot. Now, you have to understand Tom and I were living like FAT CATS. We had our own sink with hot and cold running water, generator, refrigerator, air conditioner, and Hollywood Mattresses we procured from the Navy Seabees in Da Nang.

I guess the word got back to the Colonel that our living conditions were getting a little on the comfortable side, so he decided to pay us a visit. When the Colonel walked in I greeted him and he started walking around checking out the sink, horseshoe bar, two pool tablets, and refrigerator.

His remarks were, "Mister, it appears you are comfortable but what would you do if we had a mortar attack?" I replied by kicking open a trap door, which led down under the trailer. He just shook his head and started to walk out. He stopped, looked in the trailer and saw the air conditioner. He said, "That air conditioner really does not work does it?" I proudly replied, "Yes sir, it maintains a temperature of 65 degrees." He shook his head again and walked out. Later, my company commander came to Tom and me and explained how unhappy the Colonel was. Here we were sleeping in a trailer, with air conditioning, and comfortable beds while the full bird Colonel was sleeping in a bunker with a sleeping bag on a cot. The major said, "The two of you had better figure out something to please the Colonel."

We put our heads together and thought how much our Colonel would love a nice mattress to sleep on. So we made a trip to Da Nang to see our Navy Seabee friends. We explained our situation and they had no problem helping us out. We delivered the Hollywood Mattress to the Colonel's bunker. Since he was not there we decided to make up his new bed for him.

The next time I saw the Colonel, it was nine or ten years later and he was a retired General. It does not stop there, because now, he was my boss in the civilian world with both of us working for Bell Helicopter International in Iran. It's a small world, so do not burn your bridges.

RON MCINTOSH

Ron became my roommate after Tom died. He was the maintenance officer that replaced Tom. Ron was hard to figure out and almost impossible to get close to. In fact, he explained how he and his family were not close. It was not that they did not get along. It was just the family did not practice love and togetherness as my family did.

Ron met his wife on a bet. He and a friend were walking down the sidewalk when they noticed a lady walking down the other side of the street. Ron's friend said, "I will bet you five bucks you cannot get a date with that lady." Ron crossed the street and approached her and said, "That guy across the street bet me five bucks that I could not get a date with you and I am sure you do not want him to get my five bucks, do you?" Course not, she replied and their relationship started. Now it has been over 30 years since I heard this, so the story may be off a little but still accurate.

Ron and I remained roommates until I returned from Rest and Recreation in Hawaii. After I returned, I learned that the major had traded my truck for a jeep. The 2nd brigade of the 1st Cavalry were preparing to move south, just north of Saigon in a place called Phu Vinh .

Ron and I did not have much time to unload all our assets. Captains and sergeants moving in from another unit all wanted our fully-equipped trailer. Knowing we were unable to take any non-issued items with us, they proceeded to offer jeeps, Thompson sub-machine guns, and other stuff we could not use; so we just left it for them to fight over.

The last thing I remember about Ron was when we were at Quang Loi, and a transportation company moved out. They had terrific bunkers. Since Ron and I had only a week to go in Vietnam, we decided to move into one of those vacated bunkers. The bunkers had a door on each end and you could lock and secure them from the inside. They were built with permanent bunkbeds so I took the top bunk. While I was checking it out I noticed how well built it was. It even had air vents that were in the roof overhang. These vents were more important than I realized because on this particular night we had a full moon. At some point I woke up and looked down and out the air vent and counted 14 pairs of Ho Chi Minh racing slicks (sandals the enemy wore) go by. Let me tell you, I could have reached out and touched them.

My heart started beating so hard I was afraid they were going to hear it. Well, I laid still until after daylight and then I told Ron about what I saw. Of course, he thought I had been hallucinating. However, after we got up and came out of the bunker everybody was dressed in full gear with weapons walking around. We asked what was going on, they replied, "Where have you guys been? We have had enemy inside the perimeter since 4 a.m. They caught them trying to blow up the helicopters." Nuts--huh? I am glad my heart did not ring like a bell.

It was many years later when I saw Ron McIntosh again and it was on T.V. It seems he was in some type of jailbreak with the use of a helicopter. I understand he got away, but later was caught in a jewelry store trying to buy his girlfriend an engagement ring.

JOHN S.

You know, some people create their own luck while others create their own misfortune and feel lucky when everything turns out good for them.

This is a story of one of our pilots. I will not mention his last name. However, I did see him again 12 years later in Houston, Texas, where he was a mechanic for Evergreen Helicopters. John was one of our scout pilots and the only person I know who survived flying into a group of powerlines. There were three wires and he hit them so exactly they all broke at the same time, and the only affect on John and the helicopter was it slowed him down a little bit but he kept on going. He did come back bragging about it, though.

The next brilliant thing I remember about John is the game some of the others played. It was flying fast and low, seeing how close they could come to bicycles and motorbikes. I remember this like it was yesterday; John was returning from a mission and he decided he would see how close he could get to a South Vietnamese soldier on a motor bike. This was a friendly; however, I do not know what happened, but John got too close and hit the soldier in the head while flying at a high speed.

After he landed and inspected the damaged skid with blood and hair on it, he realized he was in a heap of trouble and he was worried. Now, here comes his luck. The aircraft's airtime required major maintenance and had to be taken to Vung Tau (voom tow, as in towel), where they performed this high echelon maintenance. So, the next morning the maintenance officer got up early and took the helicopter to Vung Tau. Within 30 minutes after he left, the Military Police were doing an investigation over the dead soldier and were going around checking all the skids for dents and blood. To top all this off, while the helicopter was at Vung Tau the maintenance people just went ahead and changed out the skid, doing away with the evidence.

HOT LEG

Most pilots in Vietnam were always trying to be prepared in case they got shot down or had to land in a situation where they would have to use their survival training. I was no different. I was always thinking of ideas that would help me if I was put in that situation. I did not smoke and did not need a cigarette lighter except, for an emergency, I carried one just in case. Lighter fluid was not available, so I was told to just fill the lighter with JP-4 (jet fuel), which I did. Jerry and I had just left the refueling point and he was hovering down the runway at Quang Loi. When I started yelling, "Land! land! land!" and he did. I jumped out of the helicopter and pulled down my pants right there in front of God and everybody. Then I started spitting on my right thigh until the crew chief could get me some water to rinse it. You probably know what happened. Yep, that jet fuel in that lighter leaked out and started burning my leg. I know if it had been a few minutes longer I would have had a big blister.

Wow, I am just glad we were in a secure place, could land, and put some water on the situation. I have no idea what I would have done if we were at 2500 feet over enemy territory.

KING COBRA

Some mornings it was really difficult to rise before daylight to get ready to go on the first-light reconnaissance. During this early morning flight we were able to see smoke coming up through the triple canopy jungle layers from the fires the enemy used to cook breakfast. Occasionally, we would be able to call in artillery on their position. Other things of interest would be sandal tracks or banana leaves they used to wrap their bread.

We often saw things that would startle us. On this one occasion, I was following a path down through some low-growing bushes looking for tracks and leaves. I was about three feet above the bushes and probably going thirty knots. I was moving my eyes from side-to-side, up and down, trying not to miss any signs. Imagine, when I turned my head back to the front, there at head high I was looking through the helicopter bubble into the eyes of this huge King Cobra. He had his neck all hooded out and was ready to strike me. I do not know if he hit the bubble or not, but at the speed I was going he just fell over backwards. Because of the ground cover and the time I needed to turn around, the snake disappeared into the jungle.

Very few people have looked a King Cobra in the eyes and lived to tell about it. Oh yes, he had vertical pupils, and my door-gunner and I both agreed he was at least twenty feet long.

MID-AIR

One of the worst accidents I have witnessed in my life occurred one afternoon when we were coming home from another flight to Da Nang for a visit to the PX (post exchange). Different aircraft used different techniques to land and depart. The CH-47 (Chinook) was used for cargo and to transfer troops from one secure area to another. It has a double rotor system with large blades so when this helicopter lifted off from an area it blew dust everywhere and blew away anything that was not tied down. To cut down on everyone's exposure time from the rotor wash the Chinook would lift off and go straight up for a couple hundred feet before it would start forward flight.

We were about ten miles or so south of Camp Evans heading north. At a distance it is hard to tell how close objects are when they are approaching one another. On this day the visibility was unlimited and our crew watched the Chinook lift off Camp Evans going straight up. We also observed a fixed wing (Caribou) entering the traffic pattern downwind for the airstrip. From our position, with the Chinook lifting up and the Caribou descending and with all the conditions right, neither aircraft saw the other. The Chinook lifted into the bottom of the fixed wing. Both aircraft caught on fire and dropped outside the perimeter of Camp Evans. These aircraft burned so fast that by the time we arrived a few minutes later, both aircraft were nothing but a pile of ashes. Later I found out that both were carrying troops to and from processing, so they could take the freedom bird home. SAD

TRAILER HOLE

As I tell you of these events that have happened, I wonder if other pilots have had as many close calls. I know they all have had them; I would like to know how we would compare.

As soon as I arrived in Quang Loi I asked, "Where are the bunkers?" Everyone laughed at me and said, "There has not been a mortar attack here in over six months. If it would make you feel better, it's right over there in the corner of the field." They had us sleeping in tents at this time, and my first night I must have been in a deep sleep when we heard incoming. I jumped up, ran around the tent, and I was so disoriented, I headed in the wrong direction.

I stopped and laid down under a quarter-ton trailer that was sitting in the field. By lying down, I was able to silhouette people running to the bunker at the corner of the field. I jumped up from under the trailer and made a dash to the bunker for cover. Just as I entered the doorway of the bunker, there was a loud explosion and it sounded really close.

Since I had been wounded by mortar fire previously, my subconscious would put me somehow inside the bunker before the first round ever hit the ground.

Many times I would be bleeding below the knees from running into stumps. However, on this night I had no warning because there were no slight thumping sounds. It was from a recoilless rifle.

Anyway, the next day that little trailer had a huge hole in it. If it had been a few seconds earlier, I would not have had the opportunity to tell you how "God Protects the Ignorant Sometimes."

KON-TUM

My flight group in the 2nd Brigade did not fly many night missions. My co-pilot, Jerry, and I returned from flying command and control all day and it was already dark when we touched down at the home base. However, by the time we got shut down, we received another mission to fly a crypto officer (person who codes and decodes communications) to a firebase near Cambodia. We lifted off and climbed to a comfortable high altitude enroute to this unknown place. We were instructed to use our FM radio and home in on their position. After about 45 minutes we made contact by radio with the LZ on the ground and immediately they advised us to turn out all lights.

Upon hearing this I asked, "How will you see us without our lights on?" The other end of the radio replied, "Trust me, you don't want your lights on. We'll listen for you when you get close." We flew a few more minutes and they said, "We hear you, so let us know when you see two lights pointing at you." Well, Jerry saw the lights and we started our approach. We were not current for night-flying and at night, depth perception, rate of descent, and closure are very difficult to judge.

Anyway, I was making the approach toward the two lights when they told me to make sure I land on top of the lights. By this time, I was wondering if this was routine. I asked, "How many aircraft have landed like this." The reply was, "You're the first." Now this is just what I wanted to hear. This really increased the pucker factor even more. We continued the approach to the lights and landed on top of this soldier, lying on the ground with flash lights held inside of used tubes that held the mortar shells when they were shipped. Now on the ground, they said, "I would not stay long if I were you." The crypto officer jumped off and we lifted off and started climbing out without lights. It was so dark and we had no reference points. Then suddenly Jerry said calmly, "You're in a dive." I pulled back on the cyclic, made the corrections and we returned back safely. "GOD PROTECTS the IGNORANT... sometimes." This flight had totally been out of our comfort zone.

ENGINE FAILURE

My co-pilot, Jerry, and I were flying command and control for the 2nd of the 7th 1st Cavalry. The Huey we were flying had just come out of major maintenance. I've always been leery about aircraft coming out of maintenance. We flew the commander to check on his firebases and landing zones. For the entire day the oil pressure was fluctuating .

Finally, I told the commander that the oil pressure had been fluctuating all day and I was getting concerned. He told me to take him back to his base and return for a maintenance check-out. After we dropped off the commander, Jerry took the controls and we climbed out over a rubber plantation.

Jerry was passing through an altitude of 1800 feet when suddenly, there was a yaw. I looked at Jerry and he said, "I didn't do that." That is when I took the controls and about 5 seconds later the engine quit. The caution panel lit up and all the bells came on. I put down the collective and entered autorotation.

The problem was we were over a rubber plantation and most of the trees have only tops at about 100 feet above the ground. The rest of the tree is all trunk. This meant if we went into the tops of the trees, we would free-fall about 75 feet. There was a rice patty in sight but out of normal autorotative glide. This is where my training came into play but this was not practice--this was life and death. I pulled up the collective and used some R.P.M. to extend our glide.

Jerry was monitoring everything and letting me know how we were doing. We got to the point where I decelerated to slow us down. We were now over our landing area. However, I used most of the R.P.M. to clear the trees and to extend our glide. It probably worked out for the best because the vertical descent allowed us to miss the dikes in the rice patty which were the highest I'd ever seen. I've seen a lot of rice patties from a low-level view and these were about eight feet high.

After making hard contact with the ground and bouncing, we came to a stop and everyone was okay. Earlier, when we dropped off the commander, we had picked up two infantry guys that were going home next week.

Before the blades stopped, those two soldiers were on top of those dikes lying there in a defense mode. Now being in the 1st Air Cavalry had its advantages. One was when there was an emergency and a "MAYDAY" broadcast went out, you had support. Within a few minutes, we had Cobra gunships overhead and a Huey slick (stripped down for transport of troupes and cargo) from the 3rd Brigade picked us up. Later, we found out that the aircraft (I crashed) hit so hard it bent the mast 10 degrees. Praise the Lord, "GOD did PROTECT the IGNORANT," this day.

LUI BA DIN

It was another long day and it was dark when Jerry and I returned to our base, after flying command and control all day. Just after we shut down the helicopter, S3 decided they just had to have a crypto officer flown to Tay Ninh and they wanted us to leave right now.

The 2nd Brigade of the 1st Air Cavalry had not been in this area very long and the surroundings were still unfamiliar, so Jerry and I took our time planning the flight. Since none of our pilots were ever at Tay Ninh, they all said fly high. We had not had many flight hours at night and did not know where we were going, so we climbed to an altitude of seven thousand feet. According to the map, Tay Ninh was located just past Lui Ba Din. It was a very high mountain where the Viet Cong had caves. They could roll anti-aircraft weapons out on rails and shoot at aircraft and then roll them back out of sight in the caves. Anyway, here we are at seven thousand feet at night flying to a place we have never been before.

Then Jerry pointed out tracers coming from the side of the mountain. I was glad it was not us, but felt sorry for the helicopter taking all those tracers. They were much lower than we were and the tracers were coming from a

91

37MM anti-aircraft gun. There was no way we could help, but we did see the landing light come on just before the helicopter went into the trees. Let me tell you that was a helpless, empty feeling, not being able to help and not knowing the outcome.

We did have a little trouble finding our landing spot that night but everything turned out okay. We flew back at nine thousand feet, most of the way without lights.

HYDRAULIC FAILURE

Jerry, my co-pilot, and I were assigned to fly command and control this day. As we were in flight on our way to pick up the Colonel, we started having some control difficulties. After we did a few checks, we realized we had a hydraulic failure. The UH-1H (Huey) we were flying normally was manageable by one pilot doing the emergency procedures, even though that was not an easy thing to do for small pilots because the pedals had to be man-handled. When you are in an emergency situation in a helicopter I would say 99.9% of the time you only get one chance to get the job done right. The emergency procedure for a hydraulic failure is a shallow approach with a running landing.

Jerry and I got the aircraft lined up with the runway at our destination and started our approach. Everything was going like we had written the textbook. However, when we reached the touchdown point going about 40 knots and all was fine, the helicopter decided to turn crossways of the runway. Here we were flying sideways down the runway knowing if we touched down in this situation we would roll like a ball. I told Jerry to get on the controls and help me push in the right pedal to get the aircraft straight. Both Jerry and I were pushing as hard as possible and we could not move the pedal and we stayed sideways.

I knew we had to do something, so I rolled off the throttle. When I did that, the helicopter snapped to the front and we touched down and called for maintenance. Just another pucker factor day.

JETTISON-door

At this same airstrip where we had the hydraulic failure, Jerry and I, on some days, would spend several hours waiting for the colonel on the side of the runway next to a large drainage pipe. There had been a few mortars lobbed onto the runway in the past and we would just run into the pipe for protection.

On this afternoon, after sitting and waiting a couple of hours for our instructions, the colonel said he did not need us anymore today. So we could go back to base. Here I am in the middle of the starting cycle and mortars start exploding around us. So I accelerated the start as fast as possible to lift off and get out of the area. We had the rotor r.p.m. and I started pulling pitch and down the runway we went.

I looked over at Jerry and he pulled the handle to jettison his door. His door flew off and I said, "Jerry, why did you do that?" His reply, "I do not know." Jerry had a lot of explaining to do to the other pilots when they all made fun of him. You never know how you will react in a situation unless you have been there.

MORTAR RADAR--built in

Following my experience with the mortar attack at LZ Jane, something happened to my subconscious that I cannot explain. I would say most mortars are fired at or about 3,000 meters and the initial sound when they are fired is a slight thump. I do not know if everybody could hear it or not, but I could. You know we inherit traits from our parents good or bad. This probably is a good trait but dealing with it day-in and day-out was no longer funny.

My mother was a jokester. She would sew my pockets and pant legs up and stitch in a note saying, "I got you." However, I guess, I missed dear ole mom, so I took her place in the joke department. After everyone found out about my sub-conscious being able to pick up the sounds of the mortar tubes, occasionally, I would start to run and everyone would break out in a run not even knowing why they were running.

Later in my tour at Quang Loi we were in a rubber plantation. Trees had to be cut to put our tents in and to make bunkers. The problem was they left stumps about knee-high scattered everywhere. I would be asleep on my cot and would wake up in the bunker before the mortar siren would sound. My shins were all beat up and bleeding from running into the stumps. When the others would arrive they would ask, "How did you get here so fast?" My only reply was, "I do not know."

A little later on we were playing football on the flight line and having a good time. First let me say, if you were not sure of incoming rounds, you would never yell, "INCOMING." Anyway, my team was on offense and huddled up for the next play when it happened. I thought I heard slight thumps, so I started running for the five foot drainage pipe covered with sandbags on the side of the runway. I was running as hard as I could when I entered the bunker. I stopped and turned around. The rest of the guys, that had been playing ball just about ran me over. I said, "What are you guys doing?" They said, "If you are running we thought we should be running also." Within a few seconds the flight line was hit with about eleven mortar explosions. Then I heard one of them say, "If Mr. Stills is running you had better be right behind him." "GPTIS"

FIRE BASE--overrun

We were flying command and control and one of the Fire Bases that was located near Laos was under the command of the Colonel we were to fly this day. The night before, the base was overrun by the North Vietnam Army and the enemy had taken a big loss.

The Colonel was telling us on the way up that his commander at the base had said they had 165 North Vietnamese K.I.A. (killed in action) inside their barbwire fencing. The Colonel started talking about flachett rounds. I had seen a demonstration using a flachett round. It is a tiny metal dart and about 10,000 are put into an artillery shell. Some people would say it was an anti-personnel round. I knew when the artillery round would go off, those little darts would come out the barrel and cover about 45 degrees of effective kill zone. Great for close battle.

When we arrived at the Fire Base there were a large number of enemy inside the outer perimeter. I do not know what size artillery rounds they used with the flachett but it actually moved the jungle back. There were bodies pinned in the trees. I had not seen this type of situation before. I took out my camera and put in a roll of film.

The only thing I have left of this scene is the memory. If the film was developed, someone kept the pictures or they were censured. They did not come back.

BRIDGE CROSSING

Now, I have done many stupid things in my lifetime but this one was beyond stupid. After Viet Nam, I became a flight instructor at Fort Rucker, Alabama. My cousin, Larry Crum, was in the reserves spending his two weeks of training at Fort Rucker. He and his wife stayed with us a few days before they left to go back to Greeneville, Tennessee. Since I had relatives there, my wife and I decided to go with them and spend a few days visiting. Everything was going just fine except we were speeding a little.

Larry was following me as we went up US Highway 411 through all the little towns. As we came out of Maryville, Tennessee, north of the city, I was still in front going around sixty mph when I topped this hill, the road turned and I lost control of the vehicle. I was sliding sideways toward a bridge and at the same time going off the embankment.

I do not know how I recovered but right before we hit the bridge, the car snapped back on the road and went across the bridge. My wife and two children were asleep and it was before seat belts were common.

I think I was protected again but I did learn a lot and I thank God every night for watching over us. THANK YOU LORD!

GAS TRUCK

You know, some of the most versatile and talented people are helicopter pilots who seek employment between flying jobs. One of my many jobs was selling insurance in North Georgia. I went door-to-door in the land of poultry farmers. This day everything was going very slowly and my attitude was bad. I stayed at it and did my best. I was not finding anyone at home, so I decided to turn around and go to another area hoping to get better results. The location was south of Canton, Georgia on highway 5.

I pulled into a driveway to turn around and I cleared myself and backed out into the road. In my rear view mirror I saw this gas tanker come over a rise going too fast. When he saw me sitting there in the road, he locked down on the brakes, black smoke billowed from the tires, and he started to jack-knife.

When I realized what was happening, I just pulled back into the driveway and it gave the truck driver enough room to recover. I backed back out of the driveway a little excited but if you drive a lot you are going to have close calls occasionally. As I continued down the road, I saw the gas tanker pulled off to the side of the road. I slowed down in case I could help if something was wrong. I made eye contact with the driver and realized he was shaking uncontrollably.

Well, I knew immediately how he felt because when I was blown off the mountain in Vietnam, I had had this same uncontrollable shaking experience.

TURTLE

My wife and I met in 1975. After a few months together, I had the opportunity to go to work for Bell Helicopter in Iran. The only condition was I had to get my Flight Instructor Certificate first.

I started the instruction and had hours of aircraft time left over after my check ride, so I decided to give everyone a ride. In Atlanta, we had a lot of air space we had to avoid and could stay out of everyone's way by flying low up the Chattahoochee River.

At the time, we were not married but were living together, so I took her for a ride first. We went to Charlie Brown Airport and picked up the helicopter and flew back to Kennesaw. Her father had a small lake on his place and he would tell about the big fish and all the ducks he would buy to put on the lake that would just disappear. He would also brag how clear the lake used to be.

When I saw the lake he talked about, it appeared to me something that muddy never had a chance of being clear. Anyway, as we were almost to her father's house we came upon this small lake. Right in the middle of the lake was the largest turtle I have ever seen. We were about 100 feet above this creature and we had an oak circular table at the house that was four feet across. I assure you this turtle was quit a bit larger. My girlfriend said, "I wonder whose lake that is?" I said, "As that is your father's house, I would think it would be his, wouldn't you?" Needless to say, now we knew where all those ducks and fish went. To this day I think we are the only ones to have seen this turtle. Everybody else thought we just made up the story.

FRITZ KOCEMBA

My wife and I first met Fritz Kocemba in Texas. This was after all the requirements had been met for Fritz and me to be employed by Bell Helicopter as flight instructors in Iran.

One of our most memorable events occurred at the Holiday Inn in Bedford, Texas. The three of us were sitting by the pool on Sunday afternoon having a few beers, and Fritz decided to take a swim. He went over to the pool's edge and dove in. He swam to the other end of the pool and back. Where Fritz dove in it was only three feet deep. The cement bottom of the pool took off several layers of his face. He didn't realize he was injured when he popped up out of the water and blood was everywhere.

The next event, I remember, was at our apartment in Isfahan, Iran. Fritz was a Bell 205 (Huey) instructor and he'd recently had a scary moment. He was explaining and demonstrating what had happened. He and his student were doing a night autorotation to the Isfahan Airport. At 50 to 75 feet the point to decelerate (flaring) the helicopter, the student froze on the controls. While Fritz was telling this story he was sitting in one of our wrought iron chairs. He began to demonstrate how he had to beat the student off

106

the controls because by this time they were approaching the ground.

While demonstrating to us how hard the helicopter hit the runway, he started bouncing around the room in the wrought iron chair. He crashed the hell out of that chair. I think the helicopter was built better than the chair.

BOMB SCARE

All the new employees for Bell Helicopter International took a charter flight to Iran. We refueled in Ireland and somewhere else, which I do not recall. We finally arrived in Teheran, Iran.

After we landed, everyone had to deplane and go through customs, which was not too bad. It was around 10 p.m. when everybody finished. Two or three hours later we were told to get back on the plane for our final leg of the flight to Isfahan, Iran.

We had been in Iran for about three hours and, at this time of night, it was still 100 degrees. There were well over 150 people on board this Boeing 707 because there was not an empty seat. Everyone and all the baggage had been inspected and loaded and we were ready to depart for Isfahan.

Then the pilot shut down the engines and I thought we might be having maintenance problems. When I saw all the baggage being unloaded and spread all over the taxi-way I had no idea what was going on. Without the engines running and auxiliary power units not available and the outside temperature at 100 degrees, it did not take long for the interior of the aircraft to surpass that temperature.

Imagine, here we are after 8 hours on this Boeing 707 with the toilets backing up and running down the aisle. There were a bunch of hot, sweaty, and irritable people and we had not been told anything. Finally someone came aboard and told us the delay was the result of a bomb threat. All passengers were to get off the plane and remain together until their name was called.

Each person was to proceed to the location of the baggage and pick out their own. After doing this you could get back on the plane and your bags were loaded onto the plane. Finally, everyone was aboard and all bags that were not identified remained on the taxi-way. The authorities thought one might contain a bomb. It turned out that a new employee checked-in his baggage but missed the flight.

JUPE DOGS

Sometime in history one of the Prophets had a bad experience with a dog. I heard one had urinated on the Prophet and because of this the Iranians had no dogs as pets.

However, they had wild dogs, the Americans called them, "jupe dogs." These dogs were big, strong, and healthy looking. If there was a weak one in the pack, the rest would surround it and all the other dogs would take turns running in and biting the weak one until it was dead. We saw this from the fifth floor of the Korosh Hotel.

One morning my wife was leaving our courtyard to walk to the place where she would catch the bus to work. She opened the gate to the street and there were four perfect specimens of these dogs standing there. I do not know what she said to these dogs but from that day forth they would be there to escort her to the bus every morning and would even be waiting at the bus stop to escort her home at the end of the day.

STUDENTS--AWOL in IRAN

We were on a cross-country trip. In the past the students would have been solo. On their last solo cross-country they all had location points where they had to make reports of position and time. Well, they all made their reports because they had all the times that they were expected to report in advance. While the instructors were waiting for the students to return, there was no aircraft in sight; soon panic set in. Later, the instructors found out the students got together and planned to take the aircraft home for a visit. That is what they did. Most of them ran low on fuel and landed. It took several weeks to roundup the helicopters and students.

IRAN--sight seeing

A Pink Cloud

While I was a flight instructor in Isfahan, Iran, cameras on the aircraft were prohibited. That was sad because I witnessed so much beauty in many natural scenes. As we passed over one of the salt lakes, there were pink flamingos that must have been migrating and they stopped for a rest. The helicopter, and its shadow, spooked them up. Imagine thousands of pink flamingos flying below you. It was awesome. Words cannot describe the beauty.

Feast of Eagles

On this day our assignment was to take a cross-country low-level flight. This was done at an altitude from ten to fifty feet. At this altitude you could sneak up on things before they could make out what was happening. All of a sudden, there was a huge eagle feasting on a lamb. I took the controls from the student and started a slow circle around the big bird. He got uncomfortable and took flight. He had to bounce two or three times before he could get off the ground. While he was in flight, my students and I flew right by the eagle's side. When he realized he could not outfly us, he landed and just stood there turning around and around. I knew he was saying, "bring it on."

The Fox

Later, on this same cross-country, we surprised a pair of fox mating. To me, this was funny because the two were locked together. The male tried to get detached and run the opposite direction. As the male was pulling and dragging the female backwards, she would reverse the situation and drag the male. This continued for several minutes and finally they broke apart. The result of this trauma left the male organ so stretched it was dragging the ground. I bet he told all his pals about that sex experience.

Gazelles Leaping

When things are the same day-in and day-out sometimes you just want something different to happen. I am sure you have been in one of these moods at one time or another. We were flying low-level, cross-country when we spotted four gazelles and decided to chase them a little. The four stayed together for quite a while and then split apart. We picked one out to chase. Here we were in a desert with no vegetation in sight and here were gazelles. We followed this one until he could no longer run. His front legs were trembling. Then I looked up and another aircraft was watching. I thought I was in trouble. After we returned and shut down, one of the pilots that I respected the most came up to me and said, "nice flying." This was Jack (Rowdy) Rowan, one of the older instructors. I heard later he had a glider accident out in Texas.

A Ram on the Mountain

  I had been told how rams could climb up the side of the mountain. If I had not witnessed this myself, I probably would not have believed it. We were flying and practicing desert landings and techniques. We were also doing a lot of pinnacle landings on the bare mountaintops. After taking off from one of the pinnacles I spotted a ram down in the valley. I took the controls from the student and descended to an altitude where we could get a closer look. Wow, this beauty had large horns that appeared to make circles. He did not even acknowledge us. He just started running toward the base of the mountain we were using for training. We were not chasing this ram, we were admiring what a specimen he was. We followed him to the base of the mountain. I thought that there was no way this ram could climb this sheer cliff. As he started up the mountain, I just sort of hovered up with him. He was climbing the side of that cliff faster then I could run on flat terrain. Another "camera moment" missed.

RESCUE MISSIONS--Air Ambulance

I started flying air ambulance for Evergreen Helicopters at Hermann Hospital in Houston, Texas in 1980. Evergreen's chief pilot, Ray Champayne (who later I heard was killed in a crash by a mechanical failure in a German Helicopter BK-105 or BK-117,) called me at home in North Georgia and asked if I would be interested in flying for Evergreen Helicopters. My wife and I had recently returned from Iran. I had been a flight instructor working for Bell Helicopter International on a Department of Defense contract teaching the Iranian Army how to fly helicopters. At the time the King (Shah of Iran) had the largest helicopter fleet in the world and a shortage of pilots to fly them. The mission and culture were difficult because we had religion and speech barriers, but we were all able to get the job done.

I had not flown for a while and I was starting to feel that emptiness you get from the lack of aviation. Pilots know what I mean when I say: flying gets into your blood. I took the job with Evergreen with the agreement that if an Air Ambulance program started in Atlanta, Georgia, I would be given the opportunity to be transferred there. They said, "okay."

So, off I went to Houston, Texas, to get transitioned into the French helicopters that they were using at Hermann Hospital. My instructor was Bob LaChance and we did most of the training in a single turbine engine AS-350 known as the A-Star. We also flew AS-315 called the Lama during the training; they both had skids.

My transition was complete and the factory training for Areospatiale Helicopters was finished. I was ready to scare some people, mainly because the SA-315B (the Allouette) was a little larger and on wheels rather than skids. There was a tendency to bounce a little at times because of ground resonance, a harmonic vibration, which could rapidly multiply and actually shake the helicopter apart. In order to prevent this, you would simply pick the helicopter up to a hover and try landing again.

After several runs to Hobby Airport to refuel and learning the "do's" and the "do not's" about the air space around Houston, they put me on the schedule of three days on and three days off. When I say three days on, I mean 72 hours. We flew over 300 missions a month. I will tell you a couple of times I felt God had to be present.

TOMBALL, TEXAS

Tomball was located about 30 miles or so somewhat northwest of Houston. It was late one night when we got dispatched to the Tomball Hospital. The flight nurse, doctor and I jumped into the helicopter and proceeded to our destination. When we arrived, we found the heli-pad all lit-up.

I circled to lose altitude and finally landed. While circling we always did a reconnaissance to see if there were any obstacles in the way. Usually the entire crew helps out. After we loaded the patient and got ready to lift-off, I turned on the landing light and right in front of me less than 100 feet away was a tower the hospital used for communication purposes. While we were circling, none of the crew had spotted the tower. How we were able to land and miss all those guide-wires and the tower is still a mystery to me today. Because when I lifted off Tomball that night, I came straight up and the tower was over 100 feet high with a red light on top; I do not know how I missed it, but I must have had help. Thank you, Lord.

SLEEP FLYING

I was flying Life Flight at Hermann Hospital in Houston, Texas. In those days, as I mentioned, pilots worked 72 hours on and 72 hours off. The flight-time limits for pilots were 8 hours in a 24-hour period. The industry had figured out how to get around the regulation, so we could fly more time in a 24-hour period.

We stayed in a house trailer next to the hospital and when we got dispatched we jumped out of bed, got dressed, ran outside, and climbed a ladder to the second floor where the helipad was. We were flying French Allouettes at this time, which had automatic starting procedures. Just flip the switch. Anyway, after going through the ladder-climbing and flying through the skyscrapers about 3 or 4 minutes into the flight, I finally woke up. I have never been so exhausted. To this day, I cannot believe I was able to do that in my sleep. The crew was shocked when I asked, "Where are we going?" At the time we were running three aircrafts; exceeding the pilot's legal and physical time limits was almost a surety. Accident rates nationwide were high in the air-ambulance industry at that time.

INDIANAPOLIS

Evergreen Helicopters operated a few hospital programs around the country. One such program was Life Line at the Methodist Hospital in Indianapolis, Indiana. This program was run very loosely. In fact, the reason I was sent to Indianapolis was because one of the two pilots decided he wanted some donuts, so he just landed the A-Star in the parking lot of the donut shop. Needless to say, the flight nurse told on him and he got fired.

While I was flying Life Line, Evergreen was negotiating a contract with Carraway Methodist Medical Center in Birmingham, Alabama. Evergreen told me that this would probably be the closest they could get me to Atlanta, so if the deal went through to considerate it. I said, okay. Meanwhile, here I am in Indianapolis; they really had a great set up here.

The pilot stayed in a hotel room on the 5th floor across the street from the hospital. Whenever we got a flight, the pilot would have to take the elevator down to the 2nd or 3rd floor of the hotel, take a cat-walk over to the hospital, then catch the elevator up a few floors, then take the stairs a few more flights to the heli-pad. Most of the time the doctor and nurse would be waiting. They had a direct elevator from the emergency room. We did not fly much at this hospital because the doctor on flight duty that day took the calls. If he did not want to fly, he would just turn the flight down; so I did not fly much in Indianapolis, plus, I was there only a few months.

I do remember one scene flight in a little town with my middle name, Linton, Indiana. This was really a freak accident. This gentleman, who was a judge's son, backed a Mazda RX-7 over a clothesline pole. The pole was metal and as the car slid up the pole, the fuel tank got punctured. The car was left hanging on the pole, except for the rear tires barely touching the ground.

I would have probably done the same thing that this guy did. He gave it the gas and tried to get off that pole. Since it was dark, I am sure he had no idea why he was smelling gas. The tires spinning on the ground got so hot they ignited the gasoline and there was a horrible flash fire. When we arrived he was still sitting in the car with both hands holding the steering wheel. There was no hope.

CARRAWAY METHODIST
MEDICAL CENTER

In November of 1980, Evergreen got the contract worked out with Carraway Hospital and they named the program Life Saver. Our first chief pilot made some off-the-wall remarks to the flight nurses before we even began flying missions. The remark had heavy sexual overtones about oil rubdowns. Ha! He did not last long. They ran Tom out of town.

Brooks then became the chief pilot and eventually went on to be the director of the program. I stayed with Life Saver for almost 15 years and during that time I had close to 4,000 flights. Some of them were very interesting and I will share a few with you.

DORA, ALABAMA--House Fire

It was after midnight when this call came in: a person had been burned in a house fire. This happened many years ago. This is the way I understand that it happened.

An Alabama Power employee went home after work and when he arrives his house is on fire. The first thing that crosses his mind is his family. He runs into the burning house and finds nobody at home. By now the fire is so fierce and he is on fire. He ran and jumped through a plate glass picture window. Not only is he on fire, but cut all to hell after going through the window.

Luckily, a couple of teenagers happened by and assisted him by putting out the fire on him and getting help. This flight was very close to the beginning of Life Saver. I can remember the man was either a relative or neighbor of Chief Myers, who was the retired Police Chief of Birmingham, now head of Carraway's security. Anyway, I landed and picked this gentleman up and we rushed him to the burn center at the University of Alabama in Birmingham.

A few days later, I had a flight past this burned house and saw all the power lines around the house. I had not seen them that night. It was probably a good thing because I would have refused to land there in the daytime. TIGHT.

After the Alabama Power employee recovered. although he had a few body parts missing, the power company gave him a job in public relations. Cheryl, our Life Saver Program Coordinator, after meeting this gentleman at an Alabama Power safety get-together, told me about this guy. He was giving a testimonial speech at a church in North Georgia regarding his experience about the fire and his ride on Life Saver. He expressed a desire to meet the pilot who took him to the hospital, but never had the opportunity to do so. This was cruel. A man stood up in the church congregation and said, "I am that pilot."

I have no idea how it made this Alabama Power employee feel, but to this day, he still has not met the Life Saver pilot face-to-face. I have seen the employee's picture in some of the power company's safety bulletins.

WRECK ON RAILROAD TRACKS

THE DYNAMIC DUO

Dr. Shaw and Jim Stills

Over the years at Life Saver I worked with many doctors. One was Doctor Ron Shaw, a short, fat doctor always scratching his genitals. I remember when he was trying to cut back on his eating. He would pour all the chocolate chip cookies on the table and then pick out the cookies with the most chips. He loved scene flights with a lot of blood and limbs lying around.

I can remember one scene flight with Dr. Shaw south of Birmingham on I-59, around Calera. It seems this gentleman was on his way home from work sometime after midnight and fell asleep. He drove between the interstate lanes, then between two bridges and fell about 100 feet down on the railroad tracks.

The railroad must have had a sensor device because the safety engineer for the railroad is the one that called in the wreck. He said, "There is something on the tracks." He was correct because this guy was driving an old 1955 Oldsmobile and those cars were built like tanks.

Upon arriving at the scene and having to park on the top of the embankment I got out and helped Connie, the flight nurse, down the hill. It was covered with rip-rap (8-12 inch diameter rock). When Connie and I finally made it down and to the car, we found the patient was pinned in without a seat belt.

It appeared that the only damage to him was a broken foot. Connie asked where the doctor was and I said

I had not seen him. I looked up at the helicopter and with the landing lights on, I could see the silhouette of the doctor. We could not make it up that hill with a stretcher, so they loaded the patient on the back of a railroad truck.

I was to meet them at the next crossing a quarter of a mile down the track. The doctor and I got in the helicopter and went to the crossing. On the way, I asked him why he did not come down to the wreck? Dr. Shaw said something like, "Have you ever seen a person after they have rolled down a 100-foot cliff of rock?" That did strike me as funny.

By this time we were landing at the next crossing. We loaded the patient and as I was going around the helicopter to get in, I looked up to check for wires. Yep, there they were, about three or four wires directly over the helicopter. Now, wires on approach at night are very hard to see because they are black and so is the pavement. I had to back the helicopter out from under those wires before I could climb out for our return flight. My question is, "If those wires were directly overhead, how did I not see or hit them?" "GPTIS"

BROKEN CABLE

This is a another flight with Dr. Shaw and his bedside manners; well, he did not have any. On this scene flight (landing the helicopter at the location of the accident), we went out to a strip-mine located to the northwest of Birmingham. If you have never had the opportunity, try to land in dust or coal dust six inches deep.

I am afraid I may not be able to get it detailed enough to make it understandable. I had taught desert landings in Iran and for eighty to ninety percent of the time while looking through the chin bubble you would have ground contact. You would still have to continue the approach to the ground. If you tried to stop or terminate at a hover, you would more than likely get vertigo and crash. In coal dust you do not see the ground, so you just continue your descent until you are able to plant the helicopter. It is kind of hard, sort of a controlled crash landing.

Anyway, we landed in the dust at this strip mine. The doctor and nurse jumped out of the helicopter and ran over to the body lying on the ground. The man had been operating a dragline. Some of the buckets they use are so large you could put a bunch of pick-up trucks in them. The cable to the bucket is about two to four inches thick. While this guy was operating the dragline the cable snapped and came apart causing pieces of wire to fly through the air. Most of this type of equipment, I think, is supposed to have a protective shield in front of the operator. This one did not and the man was hit with one piece. You would think the odds of it going through the center of his heart would have been impossible but it did.

Dr. Shaw walked over to the man, looked down and said, "He is dead--there's no reason to transport him." So we left the body and went back to the hospital.

STABBED IN THE HEART

One of our doctors whom I really liked was Dr. Michael Brewer. He was fun to fly with and was always coming up with off-the-wall sayings I had never heard before. Previously, Dr. Brewer was a schoolteacher.

One day he just could not take brain-dead teenagers anymore. He stepped back and looked at himself and asked, "Brewer, what the hell are you wasting your time for; these kids do not want to learn." So he went to medical school.

We received this call around midnight from the Shelby County Hospital, south of Birmingham near Pelham. We landed and Dr. Brewer and the flight nurse went into the emergency room.

After I shut down the helicopter I went into the emergency room and started to watch a real doctor from Birmingham work. Dr Brewer realized the guy was stabbed through the heart and all the blood they were putting in this patient was being pumped out. So he figured the only thing he could do was crack open the chest and check the damage to the heart.

Dr. Brewer was surrounded by spectators and everybody was standing in blood. I mean blood was everywhere by this time; Dr. Brewer had the heart in his hand. After examining it he decided to stitch up the hole in the heart.

After he finished with the stitch-work and the heart stopped pumping all the blood out, it appeared like the doctor had actually saved this dude's life. After placing the heart back in the chest and closing the chest cavity, the good doctor realized he had sown his glove to the heart. The man did not have enough blood in his system to live. It was a great experience watching the doctor work.

BURIED ALIVE

It was early afternoon when we were dispatched to a mining accident at one of the largest strip mines in the area.

The helicopter was running, the flight nurse was already aboard and we were waiting for the doctor. The doctor finally got in and we lifted off. No sooner had we gotten off the ground when Dr. Brewer started complaining and moaning about the 100-dollar Rockport shoes he just bought and was wearing. They were good-looking, but even the doctor knew that on a flight to the mines we all got so dirty that in most cases we had to take showers when we returned. However, this was not helping Brewer's attitude about his brand new shoes.

When we arrived at the mine, the doctor and the nurse got out and left the stretcher for me to bring. I shut down and ran the stretcher to the top of the mine. There were a few of the workers standing around, so I asked what happened. I was told that there had been a very old coal dust sediment pond on the top of the cliff at the strip mine. From where I was standing I could see that the pond had been drained. Two loaders were moving the coal sediment back from the edge of the cliff, so they could expand the mine in that direction.

I could see the sediment was about 30 feet deep, and while the two loaders were moving the coal dust out of the way, the sediment started to shift and slide. It actually pushed the two machines over the cliff and continued to slide until both machines had been covered up with the operators inside.

Dr. Brewer was a very good doctor and was down at the bottom of the mine up to his waist in all this coal dust trying to get to the entrapped operators. They just could not get to them in time. We did not transport these guys. As soon as Brewer got into the helicopter he started in about those damn shoes. He had me laughing so hard I could not even talk with the control tower on the way back to the hospital. By the way, the shoes were thrown away.

GREAT GUT-FEELING

This happened at Life Saver, Carraway Methodist Medical Center. We were dispatched to a scene flight in Hoover about 8-10 minutes south of the hospital. The call came in after midnight and I had checked the weather before I went to bed and nothing was forecasted. Birmingham, Alabama, must be one of those places where predicting the weather is very difficult.

The phone rang and the dispatcher gave me the location of the car accident. I jumped up, put on my flight suit and ran out to the helicopter. We always tried to get off the ground as close to 3 minutes as possible. Something told me this was one flight I did not want to make.

I ran back inside and told the doctor and nurse I did not like the feeling outside. For me to turn down a flight because I did not like the feeling, was not a justifiable reason. I called the dispatcher and told him to have the patient sent by ground transportation. By this time, I was being eaten up by guilt. Joe, the flight nurse, came in and said, "Damn, I am glad you turned down that flight."

I went to the window about 10 minutes after the flight was turned down. The fog was so thick you could not see the helicopter parked 75 feet away. If we had taken that flight, we definitely could not have come back to the hospital because it would have been socked in. Thank you, Lord.

FOG BANK

We received the dispatch around 10 p.m. just about the time I was getting ready for bed. It was to go to a Montgomery hospital and transfer a patient back to the University Hospital. I checked the weather.

Montgomery possibly could get fog, but Birmingham was not forecasting any, so I lifted off and headed to Montgomery. We flew about 45 miles south and we started noticing a thin layer of fog. No problem. We continued on to Montgomery. It was socked in. So we turned around and headed back to the hospital.

I have heard of heavy-duty fog banks but this one we were about to encounter was beyond belief. I noticed the solid wall of fog when we were about 15 miles south of Birmingham, but I did not know the severity of it yet. Then I heard an Eastern Airline flight calling a missed approach and requesting clearance to Atlanta. I thought, ooh boy, the airlines do not usually have problems like this. I continued on and when I got to Carraway Hospital it was totally socked in.

The funny thing about this was that the fog bank was coming from the northeast and to the west of the moving fog bank, it was totally clear. I made a turn over

Carraway and headed to the landing pad for the University of Alabama Hospital in downtown Birmingham. Now this heli-pad was located on the 5th floor of a parking deck. I landed and before I cooled the engine three minutes, this fog bank came up over the wall and engulfed us. It was so thick that visibility was less then 50 feet. In fact, the crew called for ground transportation. On our way back to the hospital the security guard driving kept passing up our turns. We could not see anything, but we did return safely.

Just a few minutes before, as I was cooling down the engine, I was listening to approach control and I heard this small fixed-wing executing a missed approach.

The controller asked him if he wanted to try another approach. I could detect a lot of stress in the pilot's voice. He told the controller, "I do not have a choice but to try another approach." I thought he might be in a fuel crisis so I put in my two cents worth. I called the controller and informed him that the Bessemer Airport was clear. Then I heard the pilot of the fixed-wing ask, "Where is Bessemer?" The controller told him about 10 miles west.

The pilot asked, "Would it be possible to get a radar vector to Bessemer?" The controller replied, "No problem." The pilot thanked me and I finished my shut-down. I always ask myself: If I had not been there at that moment, would that small fixed-wing have made a safe landing? I bet someone was saying, "Thank you Lord."

DAVEY ALLISON and RED FARMER

This story is very hard for me to tell, even though it is more than 10 years since this happened.

It was one afternoon on or around the 17th of July 1994. We were dispatched to Talladega Race Track for a helicopter crash. They requested two helicopters because two people had been injured. So my chief pilot, Harry, and I lifted off Carraway Medical Center en route to Talladega. The Birmingham Airport tower controllers were always interested in our flights. In fact, they worked with Life Saver above and beyond their duty, helping us in anyway they could.

This day was no different. The area was getting ready for a big race at Talladega in a few days and a lot of the cars and drivers were there testing. The tower asked what had happened. He thought there had been a bad car wreck and we were on the way to pick up the drivers. When I told him it was a helicopter crash he asked if I knew the aircraft identification number. "No," I replied, then he said to let him know if it was this aircraft identification number he gave me.

I did not know Allison owned a helicopter. Most of the drivers owned planes and could fly but had pilots that flew with them. Often someone who had a fixed-wing license might take a quick course in helicopter instruction. I think it was around 40 hours and then you would take an FAA check ride.

If you did not do something really stupid you were given the add-on rating. A 40 or 50-hour helicopter pilot might be able to fly the aircraft but with the mental thinking of a helicopter pilot, "if it has not happened yet, it is fixing to."

At this low flight time, even if you have thousands of fixed-wing hours, a helicopter is so different that fixed-wing hours are not usually helpful. Only the training for traffic patterns and communication with the controllers can be applied. When you have an emergency in a helicopter you do not have time to get out the operator's manual and see what to do next.

A helicopter pilot has to be able to handle emergencies and has to practice so often that he will actually think about these procedures in his dreams. Some of the incidents require instance reflexes. When I arrived at the Talladega Race Track I saw a Hughes 500 lying close to the chain-link fence.

I thought whoever was flying got a little close to the fence. If the aircraft got into the barbwire strands at the top of the chain-link fence, a tail rotor failure would follow. The only procedure for a tail rotor failure at a low altitude, unless you are at a high enough speed to keep the helicopter streamlined, is to chop or close the throttle to eliminate torque.

No one really knows exactly what happened, but I think Davey Allison was on an approach going over this fence and misjudged what he needed to clear the fence. His tail rotor got stuck in the barbwire, causing a tail rotor failure.

Once the tail rotor is no longer under power, that power will be transferred to the main rotor causing the helicopter to gain a little altitude. By this time, the helicopter is starting to spin in the opposite direction of the main rotor blades. This is because "for every action there is an opposite and equal reaction."

The longer you wait to chop the throttle the faster the helicopter spins and then the pilot becomes confused. I think, at this point, Allison just panicked.

Instead of chopping the throttle, he put down the collective with power, and he would still be spinning when he hit the ground. It would be very difficult for an experienced pilot to make a level touch-down with the helicopter spinning.

Hitting on one skid and bouncing to the other skid while the main rotor blades are making contact with the ground, the helicopter would flip back and forth until the rotor blades were destroyed. Red Farmer, the passenger, was transferred first; his injuries were minor, but Davey's injuries were more serious. Flying back, the tower operator asked about the situation. I told him it was the tail number he had asked about and the outcome did not look good. "GPTIS"

This was my 15 minutes of fame, because ESPN continued showing the clip of Davey Allison being unloaded from the helicopter and there I was. I got calls from relatives and people I did not know.

LISA

Lisa was a very pretty flight nurse who, I thought, had a terrific looking body. She would run to keep in shape. The only problem with this great lady was that she was book smart but did not have two cents worth of common sense.

One day, I was helping refill the oxygen tanks located in the baggage compartment of the helicopter. We would check the pressure in the large tanks, which we rolled out of the hangar, after they were hooked up to the tanks on the helicopter. Lisa turned on the oxygen while I was standing there holding the coupling end.

I did not know she was going to do this. I was totally surprised when 2200 P.S.I. of pressure ripped the coupling out of my hand and started flipping around like an unmanned water hose.

The coupling hit me below the belt in a very sensitive area and brought me to my knees. Lisa realized what she had done and turned off the oxygen. Thank you, Lisa.

Transmission Failure

We were dispatched to Butler County Hospital, which was quite some distance southwest from Carraway Hospital, so I climbed to an altitude of 2500 feet.

Another one of Lisa's traits was to be organized. She was always changing and moving things around. Dan, one of the original flight nurses, had spent an entire day designing and making a container to carry the drugs. Lisa came on duty and relieved Dan. After checking out what Dan had done, she decided to change it. After she spent her shift changing what Dan had done, she could not get all the drugs back in the box. Boy, was Dan upset. Anyway, it would be a common thing for Lisa to move things around. She would occasionally drop stuff in the back where she and the doctor rode.

We were flying over Demopolis, Alabama, when there was a loud thump in the back. I said, "Lisa, do not move the portable oxygen tank around while we are in flight." It sounded like she had dropped the small oxygen tank. Her reply was, "I did not do that," and then my emergency panel lit up. It was indicating a transmission problem, so I called base and gave the dispatcher our location informing him I was making a precautionary landing.

I started descending and looked for a good landing area where we could get help. I kept power to the transmission in case it became a problem, and the power just might keep it from freezing up, which would be fatal. Finally, we were on the ground. I had picked out a nice place to land where it appeared we could get help. It was the 4th of July and everybody was at the river celebrating the fourth. So, we walked up to the main road and hitched a ride to where we could make a phone call. This helicopter just came out of major maintenance and the transmission had been torn down. After a couple of hours another helicopter came and took us back to Birmingham.

When Bell Helicopter heard about the transmission coming apart, they said they had never had a star gear failure. Bell informed the owner of the aviation company doing Life Saver's maintenance not to open the transmission until Bell Helicopter sent some people to look at it. However, the aviation maintenance company went ahead and tore down the transmission before Bell arrived. I guess if I had left a wrench or something in the transmission, I would want it removed before someone else could see it, wouldn't you?

Attempted Rape

This was an incident where I felt real sorry for Lisa. She was running along this road and a car passed her by going on around the curve up ahead. The only thing I can figure out is the passenger in the car got out, after they were out of sight, and started running back toward Lisa. This guy grabbed Lisa by the athletic bra she was wearing and dragged her into the woods next to the road and tried to rape her. Lisa was in good shape and stubborn as hell, so she resisted and fought back. Finally, the rapist just beat the hell out of Lisa, but she got away and ran back to the road. She was bleeding profusely from the face and tried to flag down a car for help. Several cars passed by without stopping, but finally one car did stop and gave assistance. If Lisa had been smaller and not as strong, the rapist would have been successful. They never caught the attacker. Lisa: "GPTIS".

Vacation

Lisa and several friends were going skiing at the end of the month, and they were going to be gone for two weeks. This was hearsay, but knowing Lisa, it just had to be true. She was in the drive-through line at the bank and was running late. She was beginning to panic about being left behind, and then her car stalled. She could not get it restarted. She got out of her car and just left it right there in line at the drive-thru. She caught a ride and went to the airport.

Rent is Due

Lisa's rent was due on the 1st of the month, but she left a few days before the 1st and did not pay her rent. She had made arrangements for her friend to stop by and check on everything. One day he arrived and there was an eviction notice on her door. He was a good friend, so he went to the office and paid her rent for her. This, according to the manager, kept the maintenance crew from putting Lisa's belongings on the street.

Parking Car

Lisa was always in a hurry, and she seemed to be consumed with everything she did. Her house was located in such a way that the driveway was on a slope, and the houses across the street were lower than her driveway. Lisa was in her usual hurry one day and had to get something from her house. She drove one of those Nissan Z cars. So she drove up into her driveway, jumped out of her car, and ran into her house to get whatever she needed. When Lisa came back out she could not find her car. It seems she did not put the car in gear, nor did she set the emergency brake. She finally found her car in the living room of the neighbor across the street.

Job Hunting

Lisa was a little dissatisfied with her job and was looking for greener pastures. She researched jobs everywhere; she looked in newspapers, magazines, just any place there might be employment ads. I know she had spent over a month on the idea that she needed a new job. However, she was having a difficult time finding one she thought she would enjoy. Then one day, after all the effort she made, she came to work all excited about the new job she had found. Lisa was telling everyone about this job she was considering as a nurse on a cruise ship. She would work seven days on, and seven days off. It sounded good to me, and Lisa was excited, until Dorothy put in her two cents worth. Dorothy said, "Lisa, what are you going to do with your baby the seven days you are at sea." Lisa replied, "I did not think about that." Lisa always had all the angles covered! She did find the job she wanted finally, she became a doctor!

HOUSTON--couch

While flying air ambulance I have come across a few strange accidents, and this one is at the top of the list. It was after midnight when we received the call to go to the middle of Houston, Texas. There was a motorcycle accident with injuries. After I landed and started looking around, I saw a classy lady sitting on the guardrail all shook-up with a few road burns. She had been the passenger in the accident. Her husband or boyfriend did not come out as well.

He had a head injury, and I do not know if he ever recovered. This couple was out for a night ride when there was less traffic and it was cooler. They were on a new Harley Sportster and moving along at about 60 or 70 miles per hour. The motorcycle hit a living room couch that had fallen off of a truck onto the interstate. The Harley hit the couch dead-center and impaled itself.

The bike was in the upright position and did not receive a scratch, while the driver landed on his head.

ANNISTON--Ford Astro-Star

This flight was dispatched on Saturday morning. It was a pretty day in ole 'Bama. This accident actually started at a weight station at the Georgia and Alabama state line. An eighteen-wheeler ran past a weight station and the Georgia State Troopers tried to pull him over to see what his problem was.

Now when the driver saw that the state troopers were chasing him, he really started to run. He reached speeds of 100 mph and would not let the troopers pull around him. This chase started at the Alabama State Line and continued for about 30 or 40 miles. By this time, there were several Georgia and Alabama State Troopers involved in the chase.

Everybody that looked in their rearview mirror would pull off to the side of the road and allow the vehicles in the chase to pass. This Ford Astro Star with about 8 or 9 relatives and one baby also saw the flashing emergency lights and pulled over to the side. The eighteen-wheeler hit that Astro Star from the rear at 95 mph. By the time Life Saver arrived on the scene, they had all the bodies covered. On my approach I was getting flashbacks to Vietnam when

I went to LZ Nancy for the first time with bodies lying everywhere.

There were eight or nine adults covered and I heard that the baby was taken to the hospital by ground and would probably live.

The mess from this accident was horrible; the Astro Star was not identifiable. The car and the bodies covered an area over a couple hundred yards. This was one of the times I had to ask, "Why, GOD?"

MASH--the original root

Now everybody has watched Mash 4077 on T.V. and many people just thought everything was made up. Even though a lot was make-believe, there really was a person that organized the MASH setups in Korea.

I was sitting at Life Saver one day and one of the administrators walked in and asked me if I would mind flying a man and his wife to Guntersville State Park, so the gentleman could make a speech. Later, I found out that this gentleman was a doctor and did his residency at Carraway Methodist Medical Center in Birmingham, Alabama. It turned out two doctors took their residency at Carraway in the 1940s. Dr. Henry Holleman, the gentleman I flew to Guntersville, was the character Col. Henry Blake on MASH was based on. The book was written by another man, a Dr. Richard Hornberger, under the pen name of Richard Hooker. Dr. Richard Hornberger served with and under Dr. Henry Holleman in the outfit MASH 8055 in Korea. From Richard Hooker's book the movie and series of MASH 4077 was born; I think the character Hawkeye was Dr. Richard Hornberger.

TRUE LAKE STORIES--White Amurs

In the early eighties, my wife and I purchased twenty acres northeast of Birmingham in a community called Cool Springs.

One afternoon my wife and I were in a John Boat (small flat bottom boat) fishing, when we saw a large fin come up to the top of the water. I do not think there are fresh water sharks, but on this day I was not sure. Later, we found out it was a White Amur, an algae-eating fish that keeps down vegetation growth in the lake.

That was probably why the bass were so much fun to catch. We definitely had the seaweed. The water was clear, and you could see the bass come out of the weeds and attack the bait. We did a little checking on the White Amurs and found out that they are the fastest and strongest fresh-water fish.

They reproduce in only two rivers in China and grow to the size their environment allows. Their life span is around thirteen years. This meant that the White Amurs in this lake were old because the older and larger they get the less they eat. I called around and found a person who dealt in the sale of White Amurs. They were about $3.50 cents each and were about eighteen inches long, so they would not have to fight off any predators. We bought fifty and had them delivered.

When they arrived the Amurs had been in tanks for so long that when they were released, they stayed in a group, as though they were still in the tank. After the White Amur distributor left, we were walking to the other side of the lake and my wife said, "What is that?" A Bald Eagle swooped down and grabbed one of the Amurs and flew off. Wow. It was beautiful.

Many years later, we were sitting on our front porch having coffee. In six different parts of the lake, all at least fifty yards apart, six White Amurs jumped straight up out of the water, all at the same time and all the jumps seemed equal in height. I would say they jumped around six feet above the water. My wife said, "Did you see that?" I looked at her and said, "What?" Then, I owned up to it and said, "No one will ever believe us."

FROG GIGGING

Many years ago, when they were teenagers, my son Doug and my wife's son Sean wanted to go frog gigging. A friend of mind had a ten or twelve-acre lake and the boys wanted me to drop them off and pick them up the next morning. When I arrived the next morning they were standing there ready to go. It had been a bad night for cat fishing and frog gigging. However, they did have a night to remember; Sean being the outdoor country redneck and Doug being a city slicker.

Sean kept telling Doug how mean a turtle was and would say, "they have the devil in them," and then he would just laugh. Imagine, here they are out in the middle of this strange lake in the middle of the night with a flashlight and one gets a bite and catches what they think is a large fish. To their surprise, after 45 minutes they finally get it in the boat.

It turned out to be a forty-pound snapping turtle. I wish I could have taped the stories they were telling on the ride home. The one I remember is the turtle was coming after them aggressively in the boat; they would try to hold it back with the wooden oar, but the turtle kept biting the tip of the oar off. Then, they started discussing jumping overboard and swimming back to shore. But then they started thinking, with all the snakes and other creatures in the water, they knew what they had in the boat, but had no idea what was in the lake.

Sean said one more time, "I told you they have the devil in them," and Doug agreed after listening to the hissing sounds and the smell this turtle excreted.

MAG-LIGHT

It was the middle of July and my wife's son, Sean, and family came over from Atlanta for a visit. Sean loved to fish and hunt and was always trying to rig up a trap or something to catch more fish.

Many times when Sean came over we would build a fire by the lake and just sit around reminiscing, roasting marshmallows, and drinking beer. Sean and the grandkids had been fishing most of the day in the canoe with great success, so he thought with a full moon it might be good fishing tonight, also. It was midnight and my wife got up to go to the house and get us more to drink. Everyone else had already gone to bed, except the three of us. The night was just grand.

I told Sean, "Man it looks like a good night to fish." Sean said, "Earlier today, I put a hot dog on a big hook and tied it to the leaning tree over there. I think I will take the canoe and check it out." Sean got in the canoe and headed over to the side of the lake. The moon was full but all the trees made shadows where he was going, so it was pitch black. You could not see your hand in front of your face. Sean paddled out of sight and within a few seconds, I heard some awful noise.

I thought he flipped the canoe. Then I heard the noise flap, flap, flap, and I yelled out, "Sean are you alright?" He said, "Yes, but you will not believe what happened." I said, "What happened?" and he said he would tell me when he got back to shore.

By this time, my wife returned with our drinks and was asking what all the commotion was about. Sean came out of the shadows and told us the story. He said, "As I started into the dark a large White Amur under the canoe took off and scared the hell out of me. It almost caused me to flip the canoe. I did not know what was happening. I turned on my mag-light. All I could see was a large mouth full of teeth coming right at the mag-light. I could not tell what it was at first, and I even thought it might be a beaver." Then Sean held up a five-pound bass that was doing its best to eat the mag-light. It is a true story, but few believe us.

PRISON STABBING

You know, when it comes to Dirt Bags (sorry individuals), I have no idea why God always seems to be there for them. I was flying Life Saver out of Birmingham and we were dispatched to Talladega Federal Prison to pick up a stabbing.

Upon arriving we found a young, tall, and really skinny man in his late twenties. When the doctor asked what happened, he said, "I was holding the door open for some dude, when he started stabbing me for no reason." I do not know how many times he was stabbed, but I thought maybe thirty times.

He was so skinny that a sixteen-inch blade came out the other side, so he probably had about fifty holes. This guy was stabbed everywhere, and it turned out that not a single vital organ was touched. After two weeks in the hospital he was returned to the prison. All this at taxpayers' expense.

KATIE--spider

When you have a really stressful job, sometimes to help relieve the stress, you play a joke on someone you like. Katie was a very pretty petite, innocent lady when she started as the Life Saver secretary. Everyone helped to break her in right away, and it was not long before she was pulling jokes on us. This is about a joke I pulled on her. It started when my wife bought me a tarantula spider for my birthday a few years earlier. This spider was a real escape master, a Houdini.

One Saturday morning my wife called all excited to tell me to hurry home; Herman, the spider, got out of his cage and she could not find him.

To this day, I do not know why she gave me this spider. Perhaps, it was because I had commented: if I had a pet, I would want something different. I went home and found Herman, and I returned him to his cage.

Every once in a while Herman would molt. During this process, the spider actually comes out of the skin leaving a hollow shell of a duplicate spider.

After the shell dried I placed it in a box and took it to work. I decided to play a prank on Katie, so I put the spider's shell in her desk drawer. Katie came to work and

159

chatted with everybody before she went to her office. I was just coming off the night shift ready to go home. Just as I opened the door to leave, I heard a scream that was indescribable. This little blond came running through the office yelling and saying things I cannot repeat.

She was laughing and crying at the same time saying she would get me. Later that day, she called me at home to let me know how great a scare she had had. She told me it was so good that she had put the spider in Debbie's desk; she was her secretary.

The only problem was Katie got involved with someone on the phone and forgot about the spider. Later she had to go into Debbie's desk, and it scared the hell out of her again. It's hard to scare the same person twice with the same spider shell, but to plant it yourself and scare yourself, that is priceless.

MISSING PERSON

I was on the night shift at Carraway Hospital in Birmingham and Life Saver was dispatched to I-65 north about ten miles. After I landed and shut down the helicopter I went to see if I could help. It was a little after midnight, and it appeared as if the driver of the older Mercury Comet fell asleep at the wheel and drove off the road. The car hit a tree on the driver's side.

Here's a man who just has been cut out of a car, and he is unconscious. While we were loading him into the helicopter, he came-to long enough to ask, "How is my wife?"

It turned out that his wife, who was almost nine months pregnant and not wearing her seat belt, was ejected through the windshield.

It took about fifteen minutes to find her. She was propelled through thick brush, over the interstate fence, and was found in a pasture (she was dead). I wondered that night, how some of these accidents turn out so tragic and others, that seem to be more horrible, turn out fine.

This was an accident; if seat belts had been used, a life would have been saved.

POWER LINES

It was another routine dispatch about a head-on collision northeast of Birmingham, on Highway 79. I was very glad it was me flying, rather than someone that might not have known about those heavy-duty power lines. They went from the top of the mountain on one side of the highway to the top of a mountain on the other side. These power lines were up about twelve hundred feet.

When I arrived in the vicinity of the accident, I made contact with the Deputy Sheriff on the scene. I asked, "What about those heavy-duty power lines stretching across the valley?" The deputy replied, "I think those power lines are farther north." I replied, "We need a definite location on these power lines." He said, "They are definitely further north."

I did not feel comfortable with his answer and attitude. I turned on all of the landing lights. I slowed the helicopter to a slow speed; suddenly, the flight nurse screamed, "There they are!"

They were about fifty feet ahead. If I had trusted the deputy and not my own experience, I would not be telling this story. We landed, picked up the patient, returned to the hospital as though it was just another routine flight. Thank You Lord.

LADY LUCK--not

While I was flying Life Saver in Birmingham, we had a pilot-friendly schedule with four twelve-hour shifts and then four days off. I started doing a little real estate on the side on my days off.

It required me to go to the courthouse occasionally. I went by the courthouse after coming off a night shift still wearing my flight suit.

This was when I met Katie, an outgoing lady with a lot of spirit. When she saw me in my flight suit she started telling about her son who had been in a motorcycle accident and Life Saver had picked him up.

She described everything in detail and I realized I had been the pilot to fly him to the hospital. He did not make it. Then Katie continued to talk and tell me another story of another son.

Eighteen months after the motorcycle accident, her other son was also flown by Life Saver to the hospital. She told me the details of the accident and location. I remembered exactly how her son's car ran off the road behind a church, into a ditch, then into a large drainage pipe. God did not protect him either. Now, Katie and I became good friends for many years. Katie did like to

164

smoke though; she got lung cancer and died a few years ago.

HAIRCUT

You know this is a small world at times. I was coming off the night shift and decided to stop somewhere to get my haircut. I was not too particular about who cut my hair. The only difference between a good haircut and a bad one is ten days. I had a flight suit on when I walked in. This lady's station was empty so she motioned for me to come over and sit down. She started to ask me about my job. Then she told me about her teenage daughter who had lost her life after inhaling scotch guard. At this point I told her where she lived, and explained I was the pilot that picked up her daughter. I felt real sorry for her because her daughter was a real beauty.

NIGHT APPROACH

As most people are aware, ninety-five percent of all aviation accidents are pilot error. This is another condition that could have been fatal. I just returned from a two-week vacation and started a night shift. After midnight we were dispatched to a car accident east of Birmingham on I-20. The night was really dark and there were no reference points except the lights of the emergency vehicles.

After I talked with the ground control about the landing area and possible obstacles, I circled and got lined up for my approach.

I would have never believed I could have put myself into this situation. Here I am on this approach with no reference points. I looked over at the rate of descent, and it was 2500 feet per minute.

The rate seemed and felt fine, but if I had not believed the instruments, I am sure we would have hit real hard. If you have ever experienced a rate of descent in the daytime, then at night, it probably is hard to know how this could have been fatal. Another "GPTIS."

MEAN JEAN

Jean was one of my favorite flight nurses at Life Saver in Birmingham, Alabama. The good thing about Jean was you always knew where you stood. She was almost a redhead and had the temper of two redheads, and she was not afraid of any type of confrontation. To this day, with her temperament, I do not know why Jean would always bring me coffee in bed when she was on duty. Maybe it was because the head flight nurse told her not to do it.

Normally, by the time the pilot got the helicopter started and warmed-up, everybody was in and ready to go. On this particular flight, after warm-up I was ready to go, so I said, "Coming up," and started lifting the helicopter off the pad. Jean was still outside, standing on the skid. She tried to jump off but she fell instead, flat on her behind. She was so mad that fire was coming out of her eyes. I told her I was sorry, and that I thought she was in and ready to go. I did not think she was ever going to talk to me again, but she did. Jean was a person who enjoyed good things in life. Her father was a doctor, and I think she was spoiled as a child. One of her favorite quotes was, "If it can be cured by cash, it is no problem."

Mean Jean drove a white Mazda RX-7 and everyday she would drive to the stables to take care of her horse. One day she was on the interstate heading to the stables. Have you ever noticed the front lug nuts on a semi truck that stick out several inches? Well, this truck driver somehow got those lug nuts into the rear of Jean's car. Her car immediately spun sideways in front of the huge semi truck going seventy miles per hour. Jean's car is sideways attached to this guy's front bumper being pushed down the interstate. Jean is not visible to the truck driver.

This is the time to be praying and I bet Jean was doing it as fast as she could. Finally, the oncoming traffic got the truck driver's attention and he stopped. He was almost shocked to death to find this white car with a pretty little lady sitting inside shaking and as pale as a white sheet. Jean was not hurt, but she did trade her car for a truck. Now do not tell me that God does not Protect the Ignorant Sometimes.

SCOTTSBORO

As a pilot flying for an ambulance service many of the flights are based on the weather and forecast. It was around 3 a.m. in Birmingham, Alabama, when we received a flight to go to Scottsboro, located on the Tennessee River. The mission was to pick up a little girl who was on a waiting list for an organ transplant and to bring her back to the University Hospital where the operation would be performed.

The organ was going to be rushed by a Navy jet to Birmingham from Florida with the expectation that we would have the patient back in time.

As I lifted off the heli-pad and contacted the Birmingham tower, the operator asked why we were heading to Scottsboro. I explained everything to him about the flight. He said, "You do know we are expecting fog at daylight." I replied, "Yes, I looked at the forecast and decided we would give it a try. " Like always, the tower and approach operators went out of their way to assist our Live Saver Program. He said, "Good luck, and if we get fogged in on your return trip, we will figure out a way to get you down."

The helicopters we flew at Carraway had auto-pilots and could do a hands-off ILS (Instrument Landing System). After about thirty minutes into the flight, we started to see fog, and the closer to the river we got the thicker it became.

When we arrived in Scottsboro, there was a medium layer of fog covering the city. Over the past few years we had made many flights here, and I was very familiar with the landing area near the hospital. I circled a few times losing altitude and located the lights of the emergency vehicles used in assisting us to land.

We were on the ground about fifteen minutes. By the time we were ready to lift off, we were fogged in. I made an instrument takeoff and climbed out above the fog and headed back to Birmingham. On our way back the sun was coming up which did not help our fog situation.

When I contacted approach control, I was informed that Birmingham was now socked in with fog. This is the time when the pucker factor starts to rise. When I arrived in Birmingham the tower wanted to know my intentions and I told him I wanted to fly over the hospital to see how badly it was fogged in.

When I was over the hospital I could see our heli-pad. I told the tower to terminate radar because we were on final approach for the hospital. We landed, and our patient was sent by ground over to the University Hospital. That clearing over the hospital was the first time we had seen the ground since we left Scottsboro. It was AMAZING!

WINFIELD

It was right before the end of the shift when we received a flight to Winfield northwest of Birmingham. It was about forty minutes away. When we lifted off, the weather was clear with no forecast of bad weather. It was just as we were approaching the little town that I noticed the fog. When we reached the hospital it was fogged in, so we had to land in a bank parking lot. The doctor and nurse took an ambulance to the hospital. We were on the ground only about thirty minutes, and by the time we loaded the patient, we were socked in. I knew Birmingham was clear, and no fog was forecasted. All I had to do was climb above the fog and return to base.

I did departure using instruments and climbed out of the fog at 1500 feet. However, I was shocked when I got on top of the fog. The whole area was now socked in with fog. I called Birmingham Approach Control, and he advised me that there had been an un-forecasted weather change. The Birmingham weather was 900 feet overcast and was now IFR (Instrument Flight Rules). Approach Control asked me if I wanted him to give me radar vectors to the ILS approach. I told him, not at this time. I requested a special

VFR (Visual Flight Rules) so I could enter his controlled area. He approved the request, and I continued on toward the hospital. The closer I got the denser and thicker the fog became. When I reached the hospital, suddenly, before my eyes, was the heli-pad. I terminated with Approach Control and went down through the hole in the fog and landed. Again, I felt blessed. Maybe it was because we were in the people-helping business.

FUEL-formula

You know, with all the experiences a person has that are negative, you try to learn from them so you do not duplicate the same experience in the future.

One morning around 3 a.m. the flight crew was dispatched to Selma, Alabama. The return flight was to go to the University Hospital back in Birmingham. I checked the weather forecast prior to going to bed like always. When the phone rang I jumped out of bed and put on my flight suit. Then I headed to the helicopter to start up and be ready for liftoff when the doctor and nurse got in. The fuel gauge read 400 pounds of fuel.

After I did some mental computing, I decided we had plenty for the round trip. Our normal flight time to Selma was around 40 minutes. At night I usually climbed to an altitude of 3,000 feet. Well, at 3,000 feet we arrived in Selma in 17 minutes. This had me concerned for the return flight because going back we would have a tremendous head wind. We were on the ground at the Selma Hospital about 20 minutes. Finally we got the patient loaded and ready for the return flight.

On the way back, I decided to try 2500 feet of altitude. When I reached this altitude and I checked our

175

ground speed, I realized it was too slow. So I descended on down to 2,000 feet to check the ground speed at this altitude. Again, very little change in our ground speed.

By this time my pucker factor was getting high, so I decided to go on down to 1500 feet. At night, this would be as low as I would go. At this altitude our ground speed was better but was still slow, and my pucker factor was continually rising.

Just about all flights in the Air Ambulance Service have some type of stress, and this flight had so much stress that I started to say a little prayer. It was nighttime, there was a patient on-board and most of the flight was over forest. When we were approximately 20 miles south of Birmingham, the 20-minute fuel-low light came on. Now, the pucker factor is totally maxed out.

It was time for another prayer. I knew that the 20 - minute warning light was not exact, only approximate, and we still had about 15 minutes of flight left to the University Hospital. We finally touched down on the heli-pad, and I called for ground transportation for the crew and me to return back to Carraway Hospital. After this flight I sat down and came up with a new fuel formula. For the rest of my flight career at Carraway, I did not worry about having enough fuel. Formula example: Selma was 65 miles so I would take half the distance and add a zero, which would be 330. This would be how many pounds of fuel were required for the flight, plus I would add 200 pounds for me. So for the Selma flight, if I had left Birmingham with 530 pounds of fuel instead of only 400, I could have left the pucker factor out of the formula. Just remember, the only time a pilot has too much fuel is when the aircraft is on fire. "GPTIS"

INSECTS--ants

An officer was trying to pull over a vehicle, when it turned into a high-speed chase on a very crooked road. The officer lost control, missed a curve, and ran off the road at a high speed into the woods. Life Saver was dispatched to the scene of the accident.

I made contact with the rescue squad, and they explained that the terrain at the site was so rough it made landing impossible. Therefore, they had set up an alternate landing spot in a pasture a short distance away. Before I shut down, the doctor and nurse were transported to the accident scene by ambulance.

After I shut down and turned off the battery, it became extremely dark when the helicopter's lights went out. I knew I had to get out and prepare for loading the patient. You know they say, "watch that first step." Well, I sunk up to my knee in something and hoped it was not a large cow patty. The flight crew returned and we loaded the police officer, who was okay, just a little broken up. It took about fifteen minutes to get back to the hospital. That first step turned out to be into a fire ant mound. By the time I got back and got my flight suit off I had approximately 88 ant bites.

SURPRISE!

Flying EMS missions in the daytime was not that difficult, if you had good directions to the accident scene. However, at night there were many other elements over which you had no control, and you had to be able to deal in a safe manner.

On this particular night we were dispatched to a small grass airstrip south of Birmingham about twenty-five miles. I was familiar with this strip because I flew over it often. This night it was foggy and the closer we got to the landing site the foggier it got. Through the fog I could see the emergency vehicles waiting, so I started the approach. When we landed, the ambulance transported the doctor and nurse to the scene. I shut down the helicopter, got out and started talking with the sheriff and started preparing to load the patient. It took almost thirty minutes for the crew to return.

The fog was thicker now so I did an instrument takeoff up through the fog. Once on top I called Birmingham Approach Control and verified the weather there was still fine. It was then that I felt something crawling up my leg inside my flight suit, so I turned on the auto-pilot. I could see something moving over my knee. I put my hands around my leg to keep it from moving up any further. It stopped. I was hoping this was not a snake, but it had a large bulge in my flight suit, I was afraid to check it out. I unzipped my flight suit and reached in and grabbed it. Lisa was the flight nurse and she said, "What is it?" I took it and threw it in the back at her. I said, "THIS." She screamed. It was just a huge grasshopper.

JOSEPH LUMPKIN

One afternoon my friend, Tim, brought a person by my hangar and introduced him as Joseph Lumpkin. Joseph and I started talking and he told me he was in martial arts and had written books on the subject. He and I both had been rejected by publishers but he decided to start his own publishing company. He said he would be glad to look at my stories for publication, and a new friendship started.

In addition Joseph was interested in ultralites. This is a small motorized experimental type of aircraft. He had already been taking flight lessons until he and his instructor crashed and demolished the aircraft. Joseph then went and purchased his own ultralite and soloed himself. After a few flights he had a hard landing and had to ground his aircraft while waiting for parts.

During this time he decided to buy another ultralite and had flown it for a short time when he had an engine failure, crashed, and broke his back.

Joseph experienced a helicopter ride by Life Saver to the University of Alabama Hospital in Birmingham. After back surgery, he was up and walking again in three weeks.

Joseph Lumpkin, my publisher, is truly a believer.
GOD DOES PROTECT THE IGNORANT... SOMETIMES

About the Author

- James Linton Stills (Jim) was born in the foothills of Greene County, Tennessee.

- Moved to Newton Falls, Ohio, at the age of five where he graduated from high school. In 1964 joined the U. S. Army Security Agency and spent two years in Germany.

- Returning to the United States in 1966 spent a short time in the National Security Agency before going to the U. S. Army Flight School. On completion of flight school in 1968 spent 12 months in Vietnam.

- Returned in 1969 and became a flight instructor at Ft. Rucker, Alabama.

- Employed by Bell Helicopter as a flight instructor in Iran, training the king's army pilots to fly helicopter.

- Hired by Evergreen Helicopters in 1980 to fly air ambulance missions. First assignment was Herrmann Hospital, Houston, Texas. Next was Methodist Hospital, Indianapolis, Indiana. Then to Carraway Methodist Medical Center in Birmingham, Alabama, where Jim spent close to 15 years until retirement in 1994.

- In addition Jim is the inventor and patent holder of "The Original Jimbo Fork" an easy release fork: tailgatefork.com

- In his spare time enjoys making fancy, exotic cowboy boots for friends and relatives.

Jim Stills